The Hero of Aliwal

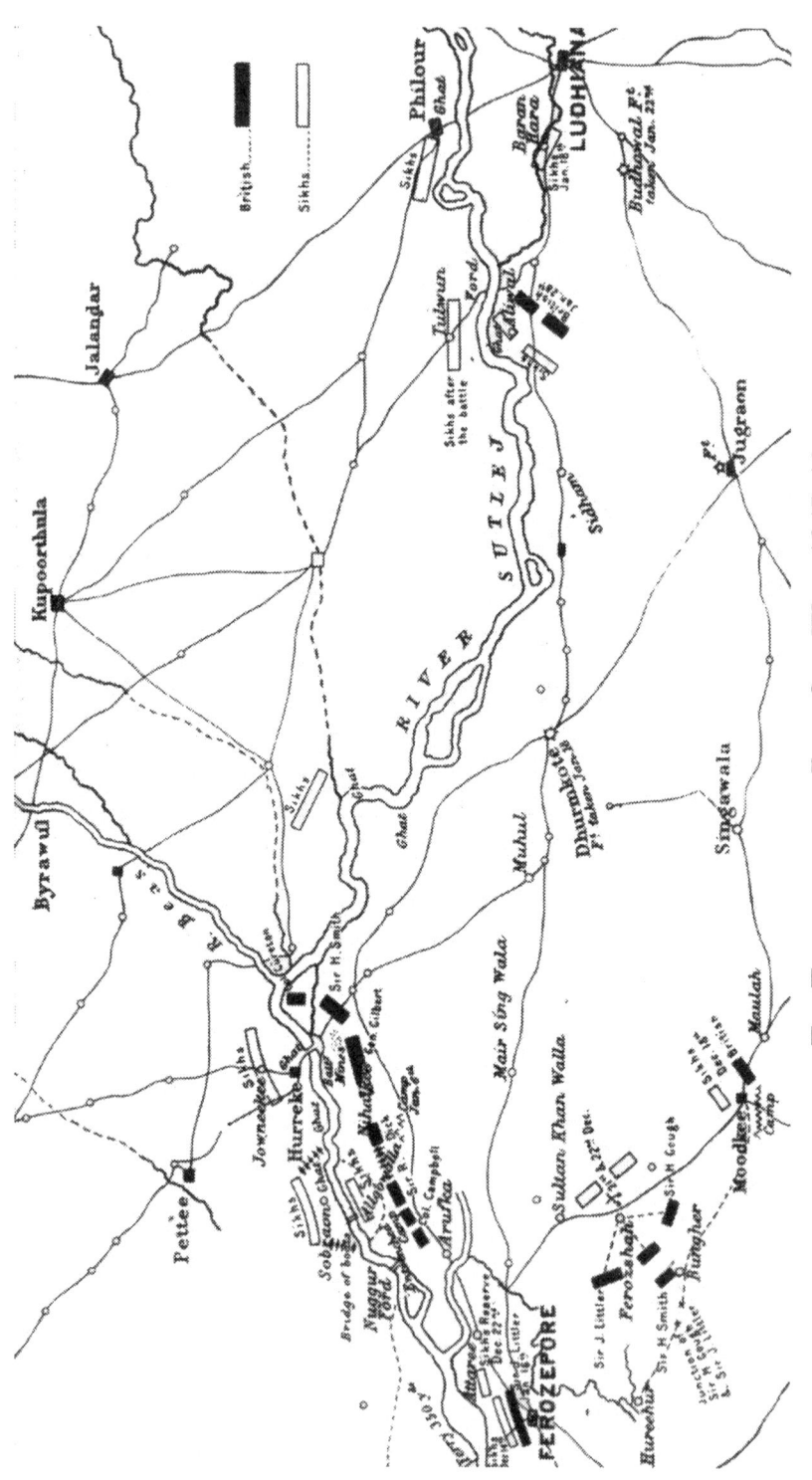

The Theatre of the First Sikh War: 1845–46

The Hero of Aliwal

The Campaigns of Sir Harry Smith in India, 1843-1846, During the Gwalior War & the First Sikh War

With a Short History of the Gwalior War & First Sikh War

by Hugh Murray

edited by

James Humphries

The Hero of Aliwal: the Campaigns of Sir Harry Smith in India, 1843-1846, During the Gwalior War & the First Sikh War

with *A Short History of the Gwalior War & First Sikh War*
by Hugh Murray

edited by
James Humphries

FIRST EDITION

Published by Leonaur Ltd

copyright © 2007 Leonaur Ltd

ISBN: 978-1-84677-237-5 (hardcover)
ISBN: 978-1-84677-238-2 (softcover)

http://www.leonaur.com

Publisher's Note
The opinions expressed in this book are those of the author and are not necessarily those of the publisher.

THE HERO OF ALIWAL
IS AFFECTIONATELY DEDICATED
TO THE MEMORY OF
'RENE' LEWIS
MOTHER & FRIEND
BY THOSE WHO HOLD HER AND
LEONAUR CLOSE TO THEIR HEARTS

★★★★★★

RENE KNEW THE HOME TOWN OF
HARRY SMITH WELL
—SINCE IT WAS ONCE ALSO HER OWN

Contents

Introduction	9
A New Post in India	17
War Draws Nearer	23
The Gwalior War	33
The Battle of Mudki	55
The Battle of Ferozeshah	79
The Battle of Badowal	124
The Battle of Aliwal	140
The Battle of Sobraon	177
Afterword	207

A Short History of the Gwalior War & First Sikh War

Gwalior	213
War in the Punjab	226
Mudki & Ferozeshah	238
Aliwal	250
Sobraon	257
Peace	265

Introduction

The name Harry Smith is a familiar one to those interested in British military history—particularly the period of the Napoleonic Wars. His name will be recognised as one of the personalities among Wellington's famous green riflemen—the 95th—in whom there is much interest as a result of the television dramatisation of the adventures of a fictional member of that regiment.

In fact, Smiths own adventures as a young man fighting throughout the Peninsular campaign in Spain and, eventually, at Waterloo against Napoleon's French Army, are almost as spectacular as the fictional adventures, particularly since he also rescued a fair maiden from danger, fell in the love with her—and married her. At the storming of Badajoz he met his beautiful young bride to be—Juana—and they campaigned together for the remainder of the war. This story—a far cry for the usual military memoir of marching and fighting—became a best selling novel by Georgette Heyer under the title *The Spanish Bride*. Indeed, Smith's own recollections of his time as an officer wearing the green jacket of the 95th Rifles appear in the Leonaur book *Bugler and Officer of the Rifles*.

Henry George Wakelyn Smith—or Harry, as he would insist on being called throughout his entire career—was born in 1787, the son of a surgeon, in Whittlesey—a small country town standing among the flat lands of the East Anglian fens—which is now in the county of Cambridgeshire, England. He was privately educated as befitted the son of a professional man of the period and it seems there was no question but that he was destined for the Army. He had an enthusiasm for military life and his notable career would prove he had a natural aptitude as a soldier.

Peacetime armies—where few incidents create opportunities for progression and advancement in rank—are poor places for career soldiers. However, Smith's early career was at the time of the long wars with the ancient enemy, now under the *tricoleur* of Revolutionary France. There were ample opportunities for the ambitious and the talented who were able to survive the considerable perils of early 19th century warfare. Smith certainly experienced his full measure of arduous campaigning and pitched battles—in South America, throughout the Iberian Peninsula, across the Pyrenees and into southern France—before Napoleon was forced to capitulate and his abdication of the imperial throne brought about the First Restoration of the Bourbon monarchy.

The great wars of Europe had barely concluded before Smith crossed the Atlantic to new battlefields in North America, where the War of 1812 was still raging with the United States. In 1814, as the fallen emperor began what seemed to be his eternal exile on the Mediterranean island of Elba, Smith took part in the burning of Washington and the battles that accompanied it—the culmination of which was the bloody British defeat before the breastworks of New Orleans, inflicted by the ragtag citizen army of Andrew Jackson. Peace was negotiated with the American government shortly after and it must have been with a heavy heart that Smith returned to Europe having seemingly crowned his years of soldiering with his part in so ignominious a defeat.

It was not to be. Napoleon had slipped his fetters, landed in France and marched to Paris across a country where the populace and the army rejoiced in his triumphant return. The French king vacated a throne he had barely warmed and the Emperor, now reinstated, desperately attempted to persuade the powers of Europe of his peaceful intentions in order to buy himself the vital time for consolidation. They knew him of old and would have none of it.

As the One Hundred Days of Napoleon's play for power drew to a close in conflict in the fields of Belgium, at Waterloo, Smith was reunited with his beloved regiment—the Rifles—under the command of this great captain, the Duke of Wellington, with whom he shared a hasty breakfast on the morning of the battle. Smith, as Brigade-major, played his own small part in the bloody battle that would end an epoch forever—and which would become the most famous battle in the world and, just as it symbolised the death of Napoleon's hope and ambition, a byword for ultimate failure. Fortunately, Smith survived Waterloo without a scratch.

It would be more than a decade before another opportunity to advance his military ambitions came Smith's way.

In 1828 he was ordered to the Cape of Good Hope—where he commanded a division in the Kaffir Wars of 1834-36. The troubles in the Cape colony were unique to the place, with the problems with the colonists—particularly the Dutch extracted Boers—compounded by perpetual risings and dangers from the tribes of the Kaffirs into whose ancestral lands everyone was pushing. Smith was not the first—or last—soldier who found that his ambitions for battlefield command were subordinated by the demands of management and administration. Nevertheless, as Governor of the Queen Adelaide province he did his best—to the extent that he appeared to be genuinely popular and appreciated by all concerned. Unfortunately for Smith, his popularity did not extend to his superiors who not only relieved him, but reversed his policies with disastrous results.

Warfare against African tribes also had its own special requirements to be effective and successful, but it is hard to imagine that a senior officer who had stood on great fields of conflict, with the 'Iron Duke' at his back and the eagles of the Imperial Guard commanded by its own great commander before him, would have found the Kaffirs a true test of his strategic and tactical ability or mettle.

His next appointment would offer to him the chance to distinguish himself as a battlefield commander that he sought. To the regret of his South African charges Smith was appointed Deputy Adjutant General of the army in India, where the British Empire was spreading its influence to finally envelope the Sub-Continent. There had been conflicts to advance British interests in the area for a almost a century, but what lay ahead would prove far more formidable.

The kingdom of the Sikhs in the Punjab was ruled and occupied by a martial race for whom religion and the army were inexorably combined in the form of the Khalsa. More than that, the Army of the Sikhs was at the time constructed, trained and equipped—particularly with a formidable train of artillery, modelled on those of European armies—under the influence of soldiers of fortune, all of whom had learnt their trade in the same or comparable campaigns as Smith himself. Many of them were formerly officers in Napoleon's army.

Smith would have to learn and understand how to fight on an Indian battlefield—and he undertook a copious amount of research to ensure that he did—for here was the potential to excel in a full scale battle, structured on the familiar lines of the Napoleonic Wars, against a courageous and formidable enemy.

Harry Smith had always acknowledged his debt in the learning of his military craft to the Great Duke and when the time came to put all he had learned into practice, as a divisional commander under Sir Hugh Gough, he demonstrated not only that he had learned his lessons well, but also that his abilities put him in a different class to his own commander—who, as Smith identified in his earliest writings from India, rarely failed to perform in a way that suffered from shortcomings that he deplored.

It is widely accepted that Smith's demonstration of generalship was a set-piece example of perfect battlefield management—by the standards of the time. It earned him that which he possibly valued the most—the effusive praise of his mentor the Duke of Wellington and the popular accolade 'The Hero of Aliwal'. Both gave him lasting pleasure and he was never embarrassed to refer to himself by the latter title!

The principal voice in *The Hero of Aliwal*—and the one that runs through the entire book—is that of Harry Smith himself. Within the pages of his autobiography Smith included correspondence of which he was the author and letters written to him by others. Since his actual writing can be sketchy, his original editors also did their part when it came to adding additional material of relevance. That sketchiness is also occasionally true of his Sikh War records.

We can perhaps excuse Sir Harry—who had a long career—for perhaps not fully appreciating that it would be his performance on the battlefield in India that would bring the fame which would solely reflect his calibre as a leader and his abilities as a great captain of men in conflict. Yet this is indisputably so, for he would become Sir Harry Smith, 1st Baronet of Aliwal as a result of his great victory.

Certainly, Smith wrote about his days in the 95th Rifles in far more detail than he did his time in India, but those were the first of his writings and told of times of youth and romance under the tutelage of his mentor, the Duke. Perhaps for this reason other writers also have concentrated mainly on his early career. In *The Hero of Aliwal*, I have tried to redress the balance, to help readers more fully appreciate Sir Harry's experiences on campaign and on the battlefield in India—experiences that included his own *masterpiece* among battles, Aliwal, 'the battle without a mistake'.

In this book I have supplemented Smith's account with additional accounts by those who experienced these momentous events with him. My aim has been to give to this period of Smith's career a more rounded perspective for the modern reader, with details of events from the pens of those with a different focus and more personal interpretation than is possible from those who saw every development—as Smith himself, in some measure, must have done—from the perspective of the larger view of overall strategy.

Here are voices from within the ranks of the cavalry, the infantry and the artillery. Here are the experiences of young officers, senior regimental ranks and civilian observers. This is not primarily a history of Indian wars or battles. It is a collection of vignettes—each of which reveals an aspect of events from an individual point of view and which combine to expand upon the account provided by the principal character. Together they form a montage of the sights, sounds, smells, tastes, action, horrors, fears and expectations of a Victorian era battlefield

For those who are interested in a cohesive overview of the events related in the personal recollections this book contains, a short history of the Gwalior War and the campaign in the Punjab, by the Victorian historian Hugh Murray, follows after the main text. Maps of most of the battles and the theatre of operations are also included.

Readers are asked to remember that, when authors' voices speak to us from 150 years in the past, the spellings used are often at odds with contemporary accepted forms. Since the writers herein have been drawn together especially for this book there may be many different spellings of the names of places and individuals. I have made no attempt to impose my own view of uniformity on the words of others, preferring to believe that authenticity is best served by leaving these variations intact. I ask you to bear with me in my judgement that this does not detract from either understanding or enjoyment of the story *The Hero of Aliwal* unfolds.

The narrative begins as Sir Harry learns that he is to leave Africa.

James Humphries
April, 2007

Chapter 1
A New Post in India

FROM HARRY SMITH'S AUTOBIOGRAPHY

In June, 1840, Lord Hill being desirous to mark his approbation and that of my Sovereign for my services in Africa, was kind enough to appoint me to the responsible, important, and elevated post of Adjutant-General to H.M.'s Forces in India; and in the very ship which brought the newspaper gazette of my appointment did I embark for my new destination, the ship waiting from Saturday until Thursday for me.

Little was the time thus afforded for me to prepare for embarkation, but a soldier must be ever ready, and my wife's cheerful exertion soon prepared everything, although our hearts were full at leaving so many valuable, dear, and faithful friends and a country in which we had spent eleven years of happiness and some excitement, and ever received as much kindness and hospitality as the most sanguine could desire.

So short was the time that my friends in Cape Town who were desirous to pay me some mark of their respect could do no more than present me on the morning of my embarcation with the following address:

To Col. H. G. Smith, C.B., etc.

Sir, We, the undersigned inhabitants of Cape Town, do ourselves the pleasure of offering you our sincere congratulations on your recent appointment to serve in a country which can, better than this Colony, reward its brave and zealous defenders. But, cordial as our wishes are for your welfare and advancement, we deeply regret that the very circumstances which open brighter prospects to you must terminate your residence amongst us, and deprive this Colony of the services of one, whose well-known and long-tried courage and abilities have been once more tested in the performance of most difficult and important duties within our own observation.

The few years which have elapsed since the most brilliant of your services to this Colony were achieved have not dimmed our recollection of them, and on quitting our shores be assured you leave a name behind you which will never be forgotten by the present, and will be made known to, and remembered by, succeeding generations of the Cape Colonists.

The suddenness of your departure prevents very many from joining in this expression of our feelings towards you; but to whatever quarter of the world your well-earned promotion may lead you, South Africa will learn with deep interest the history of your future career, and rejoice in the tidings of your prosperity.

To which I replied—

Cape Castle, 4th June, 1840
Gentlemen, I thank you most cordially for your congratulations on the mark of distinction which Her Majesty has been pleased to confer upon me, by appointing me Adjutant-General to the Queen's troops in India.

On my return from the frontiers, you received me with warm congratulations—the services of which you were thus pleased, in a manner so gratifying to

Sir Harry Smith

me, to express your approbation were of recent occurrence—but the feelings expressed by you in the address with which you have this day honoured me, prove that the recollection and appreciation of a soldier's services may outlive the excitement produced at the moment by success, and I pray you to believe that the recollection of the feelings so warmly and kindly expressed will never cease to dwell in my memory, and will be matter of exultation to me in whatever clime or quarter of the globe it may be my lot to serve.

During a residence of eleven years, I have met with invariable kindness from all classes in the Colony—I may say, from the community at large; and although I cannot but feel that an honour of no ordinary class has been conferred upon me by Her Majesty, yet I say from my heart that I now quit your shores with deep regret.

I have the honour to be, Gentlemen,
Your most obedient, humble servant,
H. G. Smith
Colonel

And the Governor of the Cape, Sir George Napier, issued the following General Order:

Headquarters, Cape Town, 1st June, 1840.

In consequence of the promotion of Colonel Smith to be Adjutant-General to the Army in India, the Commander-in-Chief takes this opportunity to express his high approbation of that officer's services during his residence in this Colony, and he feels confident the officers and soldiers of this command will be highly gratified by so distinguished a mark of Her Majesty's favour and approbation being bestowed on an officer of such long and gallant services in nearly every part of Her Majesty's Dominions.

As one of his companions, and as an old Comrade in Arms, the Major-General offers Colonel Smith his warmest congratulations and best wishes for his health and happiness.

The Orders of the Garrison of Cape Town, and of the guards and sentries, etc., as established by Colonel Smith, C.B., are to be considered as Standing Orders for this Garrison, and will be strictly observed accordingly.

However gratified we were by this distinguished mark of Her Majesty's approbation, we left the Cape of Good Hope as if we were leaving forever our native land, and in that patriotic expression "My native land, good night" is comprised all the most feeling heart of man can participate in.

Ah, Cape of Good Hope, notwithstanding your terrific south-easters in the summer, your dreadful north-westers in the winter, your burning sun, your awful sands, I and my wife will ever remember you with an affection yielding alone to that of the "Land of our Sires!"

CHAPTER 2.

War Draws Nearer

FROM HARRY SMITH'S AUTOBIOGRAPHY

On the voyage we encountered terrific gales of wind; one night a squall took us aback, carried away our topmasts, and shivered our sails into shreds in a moment. I never knew or could conceive before what the force of wind was capable of. This excessive violence lasted only twenty minutes, leaving us a log on the water. The gale continued three days, and on the 18th June, 1840, we had staring us in the face a watery grave. It was the anniversary of the day on which I and two brothers escaped the slaughter of the eventful field of Waterloo. The same Divine Hand, however, protected us, and the *91st Psalm* was again read in devotion and gratitude to the Almighty and Eternal Lord God, *"Who alone spreadest out the heavens and rulest the raging of the sea;"* and we reached Madras Roads in safety after a most boisterous but quick passage.

I embarked six horses, one of which died at sea, and all the rest were much bruised and injured.

At Madras we had many friends. The Governor, Lord Elphinstone, whom we had known as a boy, and to whom we were of use at the Cape on his way out, was then in the Nilgherries. So soon as he heard of our arrival, Government House and all its luxuries were placed at our disposal;

but we were already hospitably put up with one of my oldest and dearest friends, Dr. Murray, the Inspector-General, who had for many years held a similar appointment at the Cape, one of the most able professional men in the world, and as an officer in his department never surpassed. Poor fellow! in two years it was my melancholy duty to report his death at Kurnal, in the Upper Provinces of Bengal, where he fell a gallant victim to an epidemic disease. To his exertions to avert the progress of its fatal ravages, and the rapidity with which he travelled from Calcutta in the sickly part of the rainy season, may be attributed a loss irreparable to the service, to his family, and to his friends.

From Madras to Calcutta we had a beautiful passage, flying along the coast and passing the famous temple of Juggernauth with the rapidity with which its votaries believe they ascend to the Regions of Bliss. On reaching Calcutta we were surrounded by old friends of the army, and many civil servants and military officers of the Honourable Company's Service whom we had known at the Cape, where they had repaired for the recovery of health. Lord Auckland received us with every kindness, and his Lordship's amiable, accomplished, and highly educated sisters showed us the most marked attention, kindness, and hospitality. As to the Commander-in-chief, Sir Jasper Nicolls, we became, after some time, as it were members of his family.

Sir Jasper Nicolls is a man of very strong common sense, and very wary of giving his confidence, or, indeed, of developing any of his intentions. At first I thought he was a rough, hard-hearted man. I soon discovered, however, he was one of the best men of business I ever served, with a warm heart and a degree of honesty of purpose never exceeded. His dear good wife is now, alas! no more—she died at Rome on their return to their native land after years of travel, toil, and burning suns. Her ladyship and daughters and my wife possessed a union of hearts and feelings which gradually increased until, on the death of Lady Nicolls, one important link of that chain of union was snapped, but is now riveted in the most fervent affection for the daughters.

In the career of military life, no man can reasonably expect that so rugged a path can be traversed without some personal disaster, and so it was with me, previously one of fortune's spoiled children. Lord Auckland, from report and a knowledge of my exertions and successes at the Cape, had imbibed a favourable opinion of me, and had the Burmese made war in 1842, as was expected, it was his Lordship's intention to appoint me to the command of the troops destined to repel invasion and re-establish our superiority. I had also a faithful friend in the Lieutenant-Governor of the Upper Provinces, Mr. Thomas Campbell Robertson—a man of superior ability and acquirement, and more versed in the history and affairs of India than any man I ever sought information from except Mr. Thoby Prinsep. As I was likely to spend some years in India if appointed Adjutant-General, as I had some reason to expect, I had, when at the Cape, read thirty-three authors, made copious notes, and generally studied the history and geography of this immense Empire. This acquired knowledge enabled me to converse with such practical and experienced men with great advantage to any information and knowledge I had previously obtained.

After the death of the celebrated Runjeet Singh, the state of our North-West Frontier, bordering on the seat of commotion, and ultimately bitter war, in Afghanistan, was far from settled, and it was contemplated that the Sikhs might interrupt our communication with our troops, so fearfully extended from any base of operations, and with the country of this doubtful ally intervening. Under these circumstances, I placed my ready services at the disposal of Lord Auckland and the Commander-in-Chief. Soon after this the insurrection at Cabool commenced.

Poor Elphinstone and I had been friends for years, and I had frequently impressed upon him the difficulty of his position, the probability of an attempt on the part of the restless and independent-spirited Afghan to shake off that yoke so injudiciously imposed upon him (especially as our rupees were no longer so lavishly, so indiscreetly scattered to acquire an ascendency which, if necessary to acquire at all, should have been acquired by the sword, and maintained by the sword, sheathed in inflexible and uncompromising justice, equity, dignity, and honour), and the necessity of his ever considering himself in the greatest danger when he felt the most secure; but I must not set my foot on a field which to describe would require volumes.

The war broke out. The energy of a Wellington or a Napoleon would have saved the destruction of that force; it was perfectly practicable, as I then pointed out. The Lieutenant-Governor and I were in hourly communication; I showed the military steps we ought to pursue, and he urged them on the Government, and offered to bear any responsibility with the Commander-in-Chief. Lord Auckland was a sensible but timid man, and the Commander-in-Chief, ever most judiciously and correctly averse to the occupation of Afghanistan, was reduced to defensive measures at the moment when the most vigorous and initiative steps ought to have been taken with the velocity of lightning. The moment was lost. If time, that irrecoverable engine in war, is neglected, disaster, as in this instance, must ensue. Before the outbreak at Cabool, when my dear friend Elphinstone, from the dire misfortune of sickness, was compelled to request his relief, the Lieutenant-Governor urged the Government and Lord Auckland to send me up. I of-

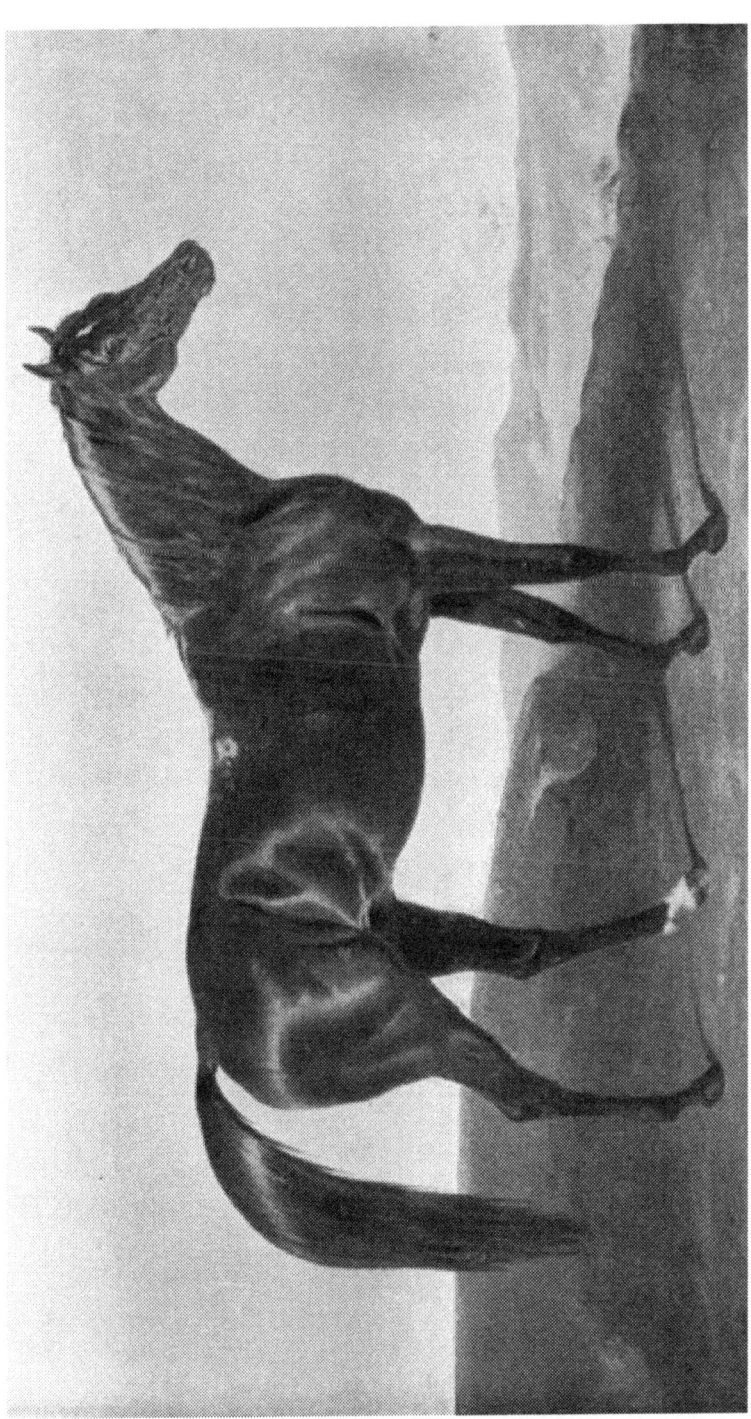

Sir Harry Smith's horse 'Aliwal'—earlier called 'Jim Crow'

fered my services on the condition that I had the supreme and uncontrolled military authority from the source to the mouth of the Indus and was aided by a civil servant; and Mr. George Clerk, the Political Agent for the Punjaub, a man of first-rate abilities and activity, most popular among the Sikhs, whose country and resources intervened between our distant operations and their base, offered nobly (for we were personally strangers) to serve with and under me.

Sir Jasper Nicolls, why I do not to this moment know, was opposed to my being employed, although Lord Auckland wished it, and Major-General Pollock was gazetted by the Government—"by the express recommendation of the Commander-in-Chief"—but only to the command of the Upper Indus, not the Lower, where Major-General Nott was senior officer. Consequently, when these two officers' forces united, they were like the *Corps d'Armée* of Napoleon in Spain, jealous of each other, the junior was disobedient to the senior, and that *ensemble*, on which success in war hinges, was lost.

The only reason I could ever suppose influenced Sir Jasper Nicolls in his reluctance to employ me—for I know he had the highest opinion of my activity—is that he apprehended, if I once got the command, the wealthy Persia would have been attempted, and my progress alone interrupted by the Caspian Sea. His thought day and night was to get back the army from its advanced and dangerous position. Whereas had the troops been rushed to the scene of action, as they might have been (for on the commencement of the outbreak, the Khyberies were with us), and Brigadier Wyld's Brigade moved by forced marches to Jellalabad, other troops rapidly following in succession, and when Wyld arrived at Jellalabad, the whole of the weakly men, women, stores, etc., been securely placed in a small *place d'armes* constructed for the purpose during Wyld's approach, while General Sale's and Wyld's forces combined precipitated themselves on Cabool, the force then would have been saved, the spirits of the troops would have been sustained by the knowledge of succour approaching, the enemy proportionately depressed.

Thus a want of exertion and decision in rendering support caused a disaster and a loss England never before sustained. It is needless here to enter into dates, number of marches, etc.; the thing I have described was a simple matter of activity and well within the scope of possibility. As soon as he arrived, Lord Ellenborough saw the necessity of withdrawing the troops from Afghanistan, but was precipitate in availing himself of the period so to do—which certainly was not at the moment when our military prowess, the prestige of our arms, and our national character for supremacy required to be re-established.

A government proposed by the Afghans should have been set up by us; then the sooner we abandoned a nominal conquest, the better for the true interests of British India. So astonished was I at the immediate withdrawal, that I wrote the Memorandum No. 1[1]. In the meanwhile the Governor-General had left it optional to General Nott to retire by Guznee, but had issued several peremptory orders to Pollock to retire. When Nott, however, proposed his forward movement, Pollock was also directed to move. I then wrote the Memorandum No. 2[2], and as the campaign developed, No. 3[3]. The moment the Afghans were assailed and the invasion pursued, they quailed immediately and did not evince the courage and perseverance in the cause of their country of the Swiss and Vendeans. If they had done so, the three divisions of Pollock and Nott and England, moving as they were upon the falsest of military principles, would have been sacrificed; but in all wars the folly of one party is exceeded by that of the other, and that which is the least culpable succeeds. This example of the want of union and energy on the part of the Afghans shows how easy it would have been to have crushed the insurrection by adopting vigorous measures at the moment.

But to revert to my own command. If the Governor-General had selected me and given me the authority I desired, viz. the whole line of the Indus, with the aid of Mr. Clerk (whose popularity with the Sikh Government and nation was so great that the resources of the Punjaub would have been at his command, and consequently at my disposal for the use of the army, which stood so much in need of them), I would have waged war upon a great scale upon the Afghan, razed his forts and fortresses from one end of his country to the other, established a government, remained in the country until order, rule, and authority were firmly established; then when the invincible character of our arms had been maintained, marched out of the country triumphantly, and not have sneaked out of it, as we did, with our tail down, like a cur before a hound.

That our national character for consistency, equity, and superiority has suffered by this melancholy attempt on Afghanistan is daily experienced throughout India. Would Scinde, Bundelkund, and Gwalior have dared to resist us but for the example afforded them in Cabool, that British troops could be not only beaten, but annihilated? The whole of the transactions of this period afford such a lesson to all Governors and Military Commanders, it is to be hoped posterity will never forget them. First principles in government and war can never be departed from: though success at the onset may attend irregularity, in the end disaster will assuredly prove that consistency, rule, and the true principles of strategy are indispensable to the achievement of conquest. To buy the good-will of the influential men of nations is folly and extravagance and the most temporary authority that can be attained. Conquest must be achieved by force of arms, by the display of irresistible power; then held by moderation, by a progressive system of amelioration of the condition of the people, by consistency and uncompromising justice. In this way the great movers of mankind, Fear and Self-interest, perpetuate subjection.

---

1. In Memorandum No. 1, dated "Simla, 7th August, 1842," the policy advocated is, "strike a decisive blow which will maintain our prestige in India, and then abandon Afghanistan, which ought never to have been entered."
2. In Memorandum No. 2, dated "Simla, 29th August," he states that his policy has been adopted. But the method involved "A division of force; an advance into the heart of the enemy's country; the siege of two cities with no positive means, one the venerated city of the Prophet, Guznee, the other Cabool, the capital; a retreat; the destruction of the base of these operations, Candahar." The plan, therefore, involved too many risks.
3. In Memorandum No. 3, dated "Simla, 7th September," he says that the evacuation of Candahar before Cabool and Guznee had been reduced was contrary to all military science. "Nott's column is now a single ship in the midst of the Atlantic Ocean surrounded by hostile fleets." "The science of war dictates that as rapid a concentration as can be effected of the forces of Nott and Pollock should be made to Guznee—reduce it, hence to Cabool. Thus the union of force ensures one of the primary objects in war—'one line of operations, one base, and a union of resources.'" "A kind of drawn battle with fluctuating advantages is worse to the general cause than if no attempt whatever had been made to 'strike a blow.'" "Our force is on the verge of winter in the prosecution of two sieges—having abandoned its base previously to the reduction of either, and it has a fair probability of being distressed for food and forage." "Our present base Jellalabad is of the most difficult and almost inaccessible character—and a whole country, the Punjaub, between it and our natural frontier." "If the enemy knew how to apply his means, he would fall upon either Nott or Pollock."

Chapter 3

The Gwalior War

FROM HARRY SMITH'S AUTOBIOGRAPHY

At this period the time of command of Sir Jasper Nicolls expired, and Sir Hugh Gough, the hero of Barossa and of China, was appointed Commander-in-Chief. Headquarters was at the time in the Himalaya Mountains at Simla, and, Sir Hugh having expressed a wish that I should meet him, I and my dear wife started in the middle of the rainy and unhealthy season on the 18th July for Calcutta by *dâk*. By this slow process you are carried at the rate of three and a half miles an hour in a sort of wooden box called a *palanquin*. You railroad flyers would regard it as slow indeed for a journey of 1300 miles. We reached Allahabad, and from thence proceeded by steamboat and found my new Commander-in-Chief. The parting with Sir J. Nicolls was as painful as affectionate. With every member of his highly educated and accomplished family we were on the most intimate and friendly terms, and he was kind enough by letter to say that he ever regarded me as a "most upright, straightforward gentleman and soldier."

On parting, I could not fail to express regret that he had not appointed me to command in Afghanistan, the only time I ever agitated the subject. His answer was, "My reasons then are fully in force now, but it was no want of the highest opinion of your abilities." I shall ever entertain the highest respect for Sir Jasper Nicolls as a most shrewd and sensible man, laborious at papers, expressing himself by letter in as few words as the Duke himself, and possessing a clear and thorough knowledge of the affairs of India and its army. In his great error of command—I allude to Afghanistan—there he was ever consistent, always opposed to the occupation of that country, so distant from our resources, so ruinous to our Treasury, but, though right in principle, he should have yielded to the force of circumstances at the moment, *restored the fight*, and ultimately given back the country to its lawful owners.

We were both received by Sir Hugh Gough and family with every demonstration of a wish to cultivate that mutual friendship and good understanding which education dictates and the good of our service and the rules of the social compact demand. We were only in Calcutta from the 1st to the 12th September, but twelve more laborious days we never passed, what with an excess of correspondence, the meeting with innumerable old friends, the formation of new, the *fêtes* to the new Commander-in-Chief, a great military dinner to Lord Ellenborough, etc., and, added to it all, the muggy heat and damp of Calcutta. The twelve days accordingly appeared to us almost months, from excitement and fatigue mental and bodily.

His Excellency had no recreation from his labours and indefatigable exertion, exposing himself to sun, wind, and weather both by sea and land in the most enthusiastic manner. Such was the state of affairs in Scindiah's Dominions, it was evident that British interference alone could establish any peaceful order of things. It was therefore not only expedient, but necessary, to assemble an army for the purpose of supporting diplomacy or of acting in open war. Lord Ellenborough intimated this to Sir Hugh, who, with his characteristic energy, sought information on all points, and soon saw his position, his resources, and the means at his disposal to collect that army which should be irresistible if compelled to take the field, or adequate to making a demonstration which would no less surely bring about the required result. To assemble an army in India requires much arrangement and consideration. There are various points at which the maintenance of an armed force is indispensable; the extent of country in our occupation entails in all concentrations particularly long and tedious marches: lastly, the season of the year must be rigidly attended to, for such is the fickleness of disease and its awful ravages, that it would need an excess of folly to leave it out of the account.

Affairs at Gwalior were still in a most disturbed state. The country was divided into parties. One of them, since the death of the Maharaja Scindiah (on the 5th February, 1843), had adhered to the widow, a girl of only fourteen, but intriguing, designing, and in the hands of a cunning fellow, a sort of Prime Minister. This party was the strongest, and was inimical to the British Government. Hence it became necessary, in virtue of existing treaties, to re-establish by force of arms that amicable relationship which the tranquillity of India demanded, as well as to support the interests of the Maharaja, Scindiah's heir by another wife, a boy of ten years old.

An army with a very efficient battery train was accordingly assembled at Agra under the immediate command of His Excellency, while a large division under Major-General Grey was concentrated at and in the vicinity of Cawnpore. While negotiations were in progress, the troops were to move on Gwalior to menace the hostile party, so that we might secure the object in view by negotiation rather than at once appeal to arms. The headquarters army marched from Agra direct on Dholpore upon the Chumbul, while the division under General Grey was to create a diversion and threaten Gwalior by a march to southward.

According to the rules of strategy and correct principles of military combination, this division of the threatening or invading forces may with great reason be questioned, when we reflect that the army of Gwalior consisted of 22,000 veteran troops and for years had been disciplined by European officers and well supplied with artillery, and thus an overwhelming force might have been precipitated on Grey and his army destroyed, for he was perfectly isolated and dependent on his own resources alone. This, however, had not escaped the observation and due consideration of the Commander-in-Chief. As we calculate on the power of an enemy, so may we estimate what, according to his system of operations, he is likely to attempt. On this occasion it was considered that if the enemy made a descent on Grey, his division was of sufficient force to defend itself, while our main army would have rapidly moved on Gwalior and conquered it without a struggle through the absence of the chief part of its army, (for strategy is totally unknown to a native army, which usually posts itself on a well-chosen position and awaits an attack).

The leading incidents which led to the outbreak of war have been so recently and so distinctly recorded, I have only to observe that the policy pursued by the Governor-General was of the most correct character. He gave the State of Gwalior full time for reflection, and demanded only such an arrangement as could alone restore the youthful Maharaja to his birthright, and produce harmony within the State and peace and tranquillity without. It admits of considerable discussion whether or not the Governor-General was justified in crossing the Chumbul, and thereby invading the territory of a kingdom he was treating with, when one of the great preliminaries had been granted, viz. the surrender of the Dada Khasgee Wala, the adviser and lover of the young widow and the Prime Minister. However, the army under the Commander-in-Chief crossed the Chumbul by ford above Dholpore, while Grey's Division entered the dominion of Scindiah *viâ* Koonah and crossed the boundary, the river Scinde, in the neighbourhood of Kohee, avoiding, however, the Antree Pass, which would have exposed his advance to considerable interruption.

The army, after crossing the Chumbul, moved into a position on the Koharee rivulet (the banks of which are intersected by small ravines so as to be impassable but by certain roads), and about eight miles from the ford of the Chumbul. The position was one rather chosen for the pomp and ceremony of a visit from the widow, the Maharaja, and the Court, which was expected in the then state of the negotiations. This meeting was all arranged, but never came to consummation. The army were so jealous of Grey's advance, they concluded, and naturally from their own Mahratta character (being the most fickle and deceitful people, and capable of any treachery to advance their desires), that while the Governor-General was encouraging this meeting, which was to be attended by a considerable body of the Mahratta army, Grey's division would move into the rear and seize the capital and the fortress of Gwalior. The suspicions of natives (naturally jealous and ready to impute evil to all around them) are not to be calmed, and the army prohibited this meeting (if the babe widow and her party ever seriously meditated it) and moved forward in a hostile attitude, crossing the Ahsin rivulet, which runs parallel to the Koharee at a distance of eight or nine miles.

I was in the habit of taking long rides every morning to make myself well acquainted with the country. When out riding on the 28th December, I fell in with a patrol which the Quartermaster-General of the Army had been directed to take out for the purpose of reconnoitring the enemy, who, according to information, had crossed the Ahsin and posted himself between the villages of Maharajpore and Chounda. The former is advanced on the plain between the two rivulets, the latter is below the Ahsin, the banks of which are also intersected by innumerable small and impassable ravines. I accompanied Colonel Garden, the Q.M.G. On my return I gave in the memorandum as follows:

Camp Hingonah, 28th Dec. 1843

Note on the position of the enemy on the left bank of the Ahsin River:—

From what I saw this morning, I calculate the force of the enemy to be 10,000 men, and he fired from ten guns of small calibre. His position appeared to be on the plain in dense masses of troops, his left resting on the broken ground of the Ahsin River, his guns drawn out in front, his right *en air*, as if *more troops* were coming up to occupy the position selected. The sooner, therefore, it is practicable for our army to occupy the right bank of the Koharee and place itself in front of the enemy's line, the better, not only to prevent a further advance of the enemy, but to enable a general action to be fought in two hours, when desired. This, however, is a single view of our army, as it does not take into consideration Major-General Grey's Division. It therefore rests mainly to be considered whether General Grey's troops should not be so brought into direct communication with the main body as either to attack simultaneously the enemy's left flank, or be so posted as to act upon the line of the enemy when *en déroute* of our main body. To do this it is obvious that the exact position of General Grey must be ascertained. If the information of the strength of the enemy renders it expedient to await direct communication with General Grey, some little delay is involved. On the contrary, if a general action be at once desirable, it may be fought by eleven o'clock to-morrow, Friday the 29th inst. To effect this, the army should march, crossing the Koharee disencumbered of the 'impedimenta' of war, before daylight the 29th inst. The distance hence to the enemy's line is within eight miles. To fight this action early in the morning is most desirable, in order to enable the pursuit of the fugitives to be protracted, therefore effective, and to ensure the capture of every gun.

The morning was very hazy, and the smoke of the camp combining with it made reconnaissance difficult.

The army marched before daylight on the 29th Dec. in three columns, all of which reached their ground with the utmost precision. The enemy was attacked, every gun (54) taken, and the defeat general; but never did men stand to their guns with more determined pluck, every gunner being bayoneted or cut down at his post. It was the same at Puniar. The result of these battles is well known.

****

ON THE BATTLE OF MAHARAJPORE, FROM A LETTER TO SIR JAMES KEMPT, WRITTEN BY SMITH AND DATED GWALIOR, 15TH JANUARY, 1844

The army did march as described in Sir H. Gough's dispatches in three columns, each arriving at its designated post in excellent time—which I freely admit was scarcely to be expected, having to disengage itself from a mass of laden elephants, camels, and bullocks and bullock carts, etc., resembling rather the multitudes of Xerxes than anything modern, and having to traverse ground on the banks of rivulets most peculiarly intersected by numerous and deep small ravines, the pigmy model of a chain of mountains, but even more impassable. On such ravines was posted the enemy's left flank; his right extended towards the village of Maharajpore, which he had filled with Infantry and ably supported by batteries enfilading its approach, his extreme right again thrown back upon the ravines of the Ahsin River, as described in the little pencil sketch enclosed, thus realizing the surmise in my report, 'his right *en air*, as if other troops were coming up to complete the occupation of the position.' If we could have caught the enemy in the state he was when reconnoitred the previous day, easy indeed would have been the victory. These Mahrattas, nor indeed does any Indian Army, know no more than to occupy a strong position and hold it as long as able, sticking to their guns *like men*. Having observed the enemy's position the day before, it was obvious to me this morning that he had advanced very considerably, and that he held the village of Maharajpore in force, which I rode through the day previous. Upon a plain, and that plain covered with the high stalks of Jumna corn, not a mound of rising ground even to assist the view, reconnoitring is nearly nominal. However, so impressed was I from what a nearer view the day before had given me and what I then saw, that the enemy attached great importance to his left flank, the line of his retreat if beaten, I ventured to advocate that flank as the most eligible point for a weighty attack. However, things were differently conducted and as the heads of columns appeared, the enemy instantly opened a well-directed cannonade, particularly from the vicinity of the village of Maharajpore, and Sir H. Gough ordered an advance. I need, therefore, only bear testimony to the gallantry of the enemy's resistance, which in my conscience I believe and assert would not have been overcome but for our gallant old Peninsular comrades, the 39th and 40th Regiments, who carried everything before them, bayoneting the gunners at their guns to a man. These guns were most ably posted, each battery flanking and supporting the other by as heavy a cross-fire of cannon as I ever saw, and grape like hail. Our leaders of brigades in the neighbourhood and in the village had various opportunities of displaying heroism, Vallant, Wright of the 39th and my Assistant, Major Barr, remarkably so, and many gallant fellows fell in this noble performance of their duty. The enemy was driven back at every point with great loss, yielding to force, not retiring in haste. A more thorough devotedness to their cause no soldiers could evince, and the annals of their defeat, altho' an honour to us, can never be recorded as any disgrace to them. Turn we now to General Grey's division. For many days before the 29th our communication was totally interrupted, and the wisdom of the route and the disunited approach to Gwalior must be tested by the fortunate result, not by the established rules and principles of strategy. Grey's dispatch is not so well written as it might have been, I am led to understand, nor does he give full credit to the old Buffs for their gallant *double allowance* with which they contributed to the achievements of the day and the capture of the enemy's guns, every one of them. The old 50th had its share too, and the blockheads in the East, who 'haver' over their wine of India's being in a state to require no British troops, are wrong: for, liberally contributing the full need of praise to the Seapoy Battalions, that praise is so rested on the British soldier's example, the want of that *point d'appui* would entail a dire want indeed, that of victory! Now if we regard the victories recently obtained over the Mahratta force, 28,000 men whose discipline has gradually been improving under Christian officers since 1803 (the days of Lake and Wellington), well supplied with cannon and every implement of war, animated by a devotion to their cause not to be exceeded—in a military point of view they are achievements in the field which yield alone to Assaye and rank with Dieg, Laswarree, and Mehudpore, and in a political point of view, their importance is immense, struck in the very heart of India, within the hearing almost of the seat of government of our Upper Provinces, Agra.

Remembering the disasters in Affghanistan, which still, as they ever will, hold their baneful influence over British India; reviewing the recent bloody murders, and present confusion and anarchy at Lahore; the still unsettled state of Bundelkund; the sickness in Scinde (that accursed Scinde), the grave of our army; the intrigues at the court of Nepaul, which have been rife and ready for mischief pending the late contest—then may my Lord Ellenborough and our country congratulate themselves upon the re-establishment of the 'Prestige of our Arms' as a sure foundation of our Indian Empire, the very base of which was tremulous, for it is well known that these Mahrattas have been *advocating hostility in every court of the East.* It is to be hoped, therefore, coupled with Lord E.'s moderation and the equity of his acts in thus re-establishing the youthful Maharaja on his throne, that our country and its Government will regard this as no war of foreign invasion, no war of conquest and unjust aggression, but one of absolute necessity to maintain the one Power paramount in India on the faith of old treaties of amity, and a demonstration to the present disturbed states of India, to the well-disposed, and to the World, that the British Lion will be ever triumphant; and that it will accordingly treat the soldiers who have achieved victories of such political magnitude with the liberality shown to *the heroes exiled* from Affghanistan, their discomfitures conjured into triumphs of valour, their miserable retreat through the Khyber Pass into deeds of glory inferior to none but the passage of San Bernardo by Napoleon. In this hope we may venture to trust a fair construction will be put on our acts, and that I may see my gallant comrades promoted as they deserve, and honoured in the manner recent services have been.

I shall ever regard this battle as one of the most fortunate circumstances of my life, if the majority of its remainder is to be spent in India, by its having acquired me that experience in Indian warfare all require, and above all, to hold in just estimation your enemy, a creed I have ever advocated, and to a certain extent, in every instance practised. In the late conflict *no one* gave our foe credit for half his daring or ability; hence our attack was not quite so scientifically powerful by a combination of the different arms as it might have been, and the defects of the unwieldy machine called the British Indian Army rendered most glaring:—its appalling quantity of baggage, its lack of organization and equipment of the soldiers, its want of experience in Generals and in officers, the extreme willingness but total inexpertness and inaptitude of the soldier in the arts of war, in the conflict, on picquet, on every duty which a protracted campaign alone can teach effectually. In this country almost every war has been terminated in one or two pitched battles fought so soon as the one army comes in sight of the other, and accordingly all the science attaching to advance and retreat, the posting of picquets, reconnaissance of the enemy, the daily contemplating his movements, both when he is before you and on the march, are lost, and war is reduced at once to 'there are people drawn up who will shoot at you, so fire away at them.' You blindly and ineptly rush upon them, drive them from the field with considerable loss, take all their guns, and never see the vestige of them after. Thus we must judiciously and with foresight organize ourselves for a campaign in the Punjaub—a very probable event—for the armies of India are not now the rabble they were in Clive's time, but organized and disciplined by European officers of experience (many French), and the art of war has progressed rapidly among our enemies, whose troops are invariably far more numerous than those we oppose to them; thus by superior ability we could alone calculate on their defeat. As it is, we calculate alone on the bulldog courage of Her Majesty's soldiers, and our loss becomes what we lately witnessed.

To obviate these deficiencies, apparent even to the most inexperienced eye, we must in the first place reduce our baggage, next give our Seapoys canteens and haversacks (a Regiment told me they were exhausted for want of water, the water-carriers having run away). We must then, every cold season, have divisions of the army assembled, and post the one half opposite the other, with outlying picquets, etc., and daily alarms, skirmishes, etc., then general actions with blank cartridges. Without this the British Indian Army will remain as it now is—a great unwieldy machine of ignorant officers and soldiers.

The drill of the Seapoy is good enough, and that of his officer, and never will attain greater perfection, but unless the officers in their separate commands know how, as I call it, to feed the fight, to bring up or into action successively in their places their command, when the attack is ordered, I defy any general to defeat his enemy but by stupid bull-dog courage. It may be conceit in Harry Smith, but if 10,000 men were given him in one cold season, if by sham fights, etc., he did not make them practical soldiers, he would resign in disgust, for the material is excellent and willing, but now, like a dictionary, it contains all the words, but cannot write a letter.

I have given you no account of the death of our gallant old comrade Churchill; he was game, and tho' not free from many errors he had virtues, and his loss cost Juana and me some honest tears.

Young Somerset is a fine, gallant young fellow who received four wounds, three severe ones, but is doing well, thank God both for his sake and his father's. As I cannot write to all my many friends, if you think this letter would amuse any of my *old comrades*, soldiers such as I aim at making, Lord K., Sir J. Lambert, Sir T. Reynell (if better), Sir A. Barnard, pray send it. Lord F. Somerset I do not name, as I know you show him all my effusions which meet your own approbation.

Juana was under a heavy cannonade with Lady G., Miss G., and a Mrs. Curtis on their elephants. Juana had this command of Amazons, and as she was experienced and they young, her command was anything but satisfactory. This Gwalior is a very extraordinary place. I have had some long rides in every direction, and the *débris* of the army of Scindiah now disbanding are as handsome, well-clothed and appointed soldiers, as regular in their encampments, as Frenchmen, and inclined to fight in their gallant and vivacious style.

****

THE GWALIOR WAR FROM THE ACCOUNT OF BRIGADIER JOSEPH ANDERSON OF H.M. 50TH FOOT, PART OF GREY'S DIVISION, PRESENT AT PUNNIAR

Our forces were divided into two distinct bodies. The larger, consisting of many of her Majesty's regiments of infantry and cavalry and European artillery, and a number of regiments of Bengal native infantry and cavalry and artillery, with commissariat and medical departments, was concentrated from the different up-country stations, and ordered to rendezvous at a given place under the immediate command of the Commander-in-Chief, then Sir Hugh Gough, attended by the Governor-General, Lord Ellenborough, all the headquarters staff, and several general officers in command of divisions and brigades, and all these marched upon Gwalior by a given route. The second column of the army, under Major-General Gray, consisted of the 3rd Buffs, the 50th Regiment, and the 9th Lancers. Also five regiments of Bengal native infantry, two regiments of Bengal native cavalry, and several batteries of European artillery, commissariat, and medical departments marched from Cawnpore and Allahabad and other stations in November, and were concentrated for the first time in brigades on a very extensive plain about half-way between Gwalior and Cawnpore. There we halted, encamped, and remained for nearly three weeks.

Our brigade was composed of the 50th Regiment and the 50th and 58th Regiments of Native Infantry, and under the command of Brigadier Black, of the Bengal army. That officer had for many years held a civil appointment, and candidly confessed that he knew nothing of the duties of a military command and much less of maoeuvring a body of men. At this time General Gray had us out daily at brigade field-days, allowing each brigadier to select his own manoeuvres. I was the second in command of our brigade, and our zealous brigadier used to come daily to my tent, and, with all simplicity and candour, confess that he really could not attempt to manoeuvre his men unless I assisted him by giving him a regular lesson of what he was to do each day. I, of course, consented to do so, and wrote him out five or six simple manoeuvres for each day, and explained them over and over again until he appeared to understand them perfectly.

He used then to leave me and to study his lesson for the rest of the evening, and so well that, when he appeared on parade next day, from memory he put his brigade through the required movements with perfect confidence and without once making a mistake, and he continued this daily, while we remained in that encampment.

During the whole of this time we knew that the main body of our army under Sir Hugh Gough was halted and encamped within twenty miles of us, on a different road to our right, and employed daily like ourselves in field-days. Native troopers, with dispatches, passed between both divisions almost daily. I never knew the reason of this delay; but it was by many believed to be caused by awaiting the result of pending negotiations. At last we again got en route, our division still keeping the main road from Cawnpore to Gwalior through the Antre Pass, with orders to examine that formidable position before we attempted to enter it. While halted and encamped on the evening of the 25th December our brigadier had a serious accident. He was examining his pistols, when one of them suddenly went off and wounded him severely in the head. This obliged him to be sent at once to the rear to the nearest military station, and I was on the same day appointed by General Gray to the command of the brigade, with the rank of brigadier. Such is the fate and chance of war, and I was delighted with my promotion and prospects, for we were now more than ever certain of meeting our enemy, the Mahrattas, in battle.

But before I go further I must mention that on leaving Cawnpore I wrote to my agent, John Allan, at Calcutta, requesting him to insure my life in favour of my dear wife for £6,000, and while delayed in camp Mr. Allan sent me the necessary papers for me and our surgeon to fill up and sign, to enable him to complete the insurance. This was duly done and the papers returned to him, and by return of post I had another letter from Mr. Allan, saying all was right, that I might make myself perfectly easy. But on the very evening of my promotion as brigadier I received another letter from Mr. Allan, informing me that the insurance office (being now confident of our going into action) had declined the insurance on my life without an additional high premium, and begging to know what he was to do. I instantly wrote to him declining, and saying that I would take my chance, as I had often done before.

On the morning of the fourth day after this, namely, on the 29th of December, we came in sight of the Antre Pass, and General Gray, with a strong escort of cavalry, having been sent on to reconnoitre, soon returned at full speed to inform the Commander-in-Chief that the pass was strongly occupied by the enemy, with many guns in battery. A halt was then ordered, and after half an hour's consultation with his staff, General Gray ordered us to stand again to our arms, and put the column in motion at a right angle to our left, thus intending to turn the enemy's position, and so march upon Gwalior. Some of us felt this a disappointment, but we soon heard that the general's orders were not to attack the enemy unless he attacked us.

We commenced our flank march. There was a ridge of hills running for miles directly parallel to our route, and not many hundred yards from us. We, quite unconscious of any danger, never thought of reconnoitring that ground, which our general decidedly should have done, and continued our flank march with only the usual precautions of our advance and rear guards, and from one end to the other (with our column and baggage, commissariat, and bazaar) we must have occupied a line of road of at least ten miles. Still nothing happened, nothing was expected, until about three o'clock in the evening, when the column was halted for the day and began to prepare to receive our tents and camp equipage. Then we were suddenly roused by bang, bang of artillery in our rear, and soon after by cavalry videttes from the rear guard (still many miles from us) galloping into our lines in great confusion, and frantically shouting that our rear guard was attacked and being cut to pieces.

It was now ascertained that from the time we changed our line of march to the left, so as to turn the Antre Pass, the enemy left that position also, and moved all day parallel to our position and column, keeping the ridge of hills between us until they came over and attacked our rear guard. The "Assembly" was immediately sounded, and we stood to our arms, and reinforcements of native infantry and cavalry were instantly dispatched to assist the rear guard, and at the same time the 3rd Regiment of Buffs, under Lieut.-Colonel Cluney, was sent to the left front over a spur of the ridge of hills already mentioned, my brigade and Brigadier Wheeler's remaining stationary with the general and staff, all ready for orders. Meantime the attack and defence of the rear guard became louder and nearer, and we could hear not only constant discharges of artillery, but regular volleys of musketry and independent file firing, and with these we could distinctly hear a heavy cannonade at a considerable distance. This we supposed at the time to be from Gwalior; but it afterwards proved to be our troops under the command of our Commander-in-Chief, Sir Hugh Gough, engaged in battle with the enemy at Maharajpore.

In a very short time a staff officer came galloping

back from Colonel Cluney and reported that the enemy was in great force in his front; on which General Gray ordered me to advance with my brigade to the support, with all speed. We moved off in open columns of companies at the double, and soon found ourselves under the range of the enemy's guns, fired from the other side of the ridge of hills, and the shot now passing over us. When we got close under the rising ground I halted my brigade in close columns of regiments, and the general rode up and inquired angrily why I had halted. I said to load, as I thought it was now high time to do so, for the enemy's shots were still passing rapidly over us. As soon as we had loaded, I advanced the whole brigade as we then stood, in close column of companies by regiments, and as soon as we reached the summit of the hill we came at once in sight of a large portion of the Mahratta army in order of battle, and were instantly under a heavy fire from their artillery and infantry. I rode in front of my column, and deployed them on the grenadiers of the 50th Regiment, the 50th Native Infantry taking our right and the 58th Native Infantry our left. All this was done in double quick and without the slightest confusion, and all as steady as rocks. I then took my station in rear of the centre, and ordered my bugler to sound "Commence firing." Up to that time, so admirably steady were the men that not a shot was fired until the order was given. But then they opened in earnest, and kept it up with the most steady regularity. Meantime, two batteries of our artillery were brought to our right, followed by our first infantry brigade, and these got at once into action, and about half a mile to our left we saw Colonel Cluney and his regiment and a battery of our artillery warmly engaged, and sending shots occasionally into the enemy's columns and batteries in our front.

By this time a number of our men fell killed and wounded, and it was now getting late and the sun about setting. A deep rough and rocky valley separated us from the enemy. My men were falling fast, and I saw no chance of driving our foes before us without crossing the valley and giving them the bayonet. I looked round everywhere for General Gray and his staff, but could nowhere see them. I asked my brigade-major if he knew where the general was, but he did not; so rather than lose a chance, and my men, without doing any good, I instantly made up my mind to advance and at them. I ordered my bugler to sound the "Advance." It was at once passed along the line, and off we went at a rapid, steady pace down the valley, keeping up a brisk independent firing all the while, and receiving the enemy's shot and shell and musketry in rapid succession.

The ground was so rough, with loose rocks and stones, that I and all the mounted officers were obliged to dismount; but with the loss of some men killed and wounded we managed to reach a clear space at the bottom of the valley. It was then all but dark, when, after hurriedly reforming our ranks, I gave the order to charge the enemy's guns, and at this instant I positively saw one of the Mahratta artillerymen put his match to his gun (not many hundred yards from us), the contents of which (grape-shot) knocked me and Captain Cobbam and about a dozen men of my brave 50th over. Captain Hough and two or three men came instantly to assist me, and offered to take me to the rear, where the medical officers were sure to be found; but I said, "No; never mind me: take those guns!" and with many hearty cheers they were all taken in a few minutes, the brave Mahrattas standing by their guns to the last, and refusing to quit them or to run, when positively ordered and pushed aside by our men's bayonets. Move they would not, until they were slaughtered on the spot.

When I was hit I was knocked clean over, and thought it was from a round shot, and that I was, of course, done for. My only care and regret was that my dear wife would lose the intended insurance on my life, and so be left, with our children, worse off than I intended. These thoughts occupied my mind until I was soon after assisted off the field by Sergeant Quick and two soldiers to where the medical officers were attending to the wounded. I had not got far when, by the light of the new moon, just rising, I saw an officer sitting under a tree, bleeding profusely, and resting his head on one arm, and with two or three soldiers supporting him. I inquired who it was, and was told Captain Cobbam, wounded severely in five different places, but still alive. I told them who I was, and that I was then on my way to the doctors, and begged the men to take him there also. A few yards farther on I met the surgeon of the 9th Lancers. He then examined my wound, putting one of his fingers in where the ball entered, and another where it passed out of my body, and then said, "Never fear; you are all right." This was indeed cheering, and enough to make me forget my fears about the loss to my dear wife of the insurance on my life.

He then ordered my escort to take me a little way farther over the hill, where they would find all the medical officers and wounded. We reached them in safety, but faint from much loss of blood. I was again examined, dressed, and well bandaged, and again reassured and told not to be alarmed, as my wound, though severe, was not dangerous. They then put me in a doolie with four bearers and my escort, and ordered them to carry me direct to our camp.

****

FROM HARRY SMITH'S AUTOBIOGRAPHY—ON THE CONCLUSION OF THE GWALIOR WAR

I was mentioned in the dispatches of the Commander-in-Chief, Sir Hugh Gough, and was rewarded with a step in the Most Honourable Military Order of the Bath, from C.B. (I had worn that decoration since Waterloo, twenty-nine years before) to K.C.B., the Great Captain of the Age writing to me as follows:

Horse Guards, 29 April, 1844
Sir, I have the satisfaction to acquaint you that the Secretary of State has, upon my recommendation, submitted to the Queen your appointment to be a Knight Commander of the Most Honourable Military Order of the Bath, of which Her Majesty has been most graciously pleased to approve.
I have the honor to be, Sir,
Your most obedient humble servant,
(Signed) *Wellington*
Major-General Sir H. G. Smith, K.C.B.

To which I replied:

Headquarters, Army of India, Simla, 23rd June, 1844
My Lord Duke,
I have this day had the honour to receive your Grace's letter, 'Horse Guards, 29th April,' acquainting me with an expression of satisfaction that Her Majesty had, upon your recommendation, been gra-

ciously pleased to appoint me a Knight Commander of the Most Honourable Military Order of the Bath While my gratitude to my Sovereign is unbounded, my heart dictates, it is to your Grace I am indebted for every honorary distinction, promotion, and appointment I have received during a long and an eventful period of the history of the world. Among the many thousands of the gallant soldiers who so nobly fought and conquered under your Grace, I may conscientiously hope none could desire more zealously to do his duty, or was ever more actuated by personal devotion or inspired with greater confidence throughout the numerous struggles of war, than he who now renders his grateful thanks for this mark of distinction so honourable to the soldier, and thus conferred by Her Majesty through the recommendation of his Commander-in-Chief, the Great Captain of the Age.

I have, etc.,
(Signed) *H. G. Smith*
Field Marshal His Grace the Duke of Wellington

Chapter 4
The Battle of Mudki

FROM HARRY SMITH'S AUTOBIOGRAPHY

In my capacity of Adjutant General of Her Majesty's forces at Headquarters (which in the cold weather moved about on the plains, in the hot enjoyed the cool and bracing atmosphere of the Himalayas at Simla), I had every opportunity of watching the gradually gathering storm in the Punjaub, until it was suspended over our heads in November, 1845, ready to burst, though where, when, or how no one dared venture a decided opinion.

Most certainly, however, no one contemplated a powerful invasion, or imagined that the Sikhs were in communication with the leaders and influential men of British India so far as Delhi. At the period when this was written, the history of the rise of the Punjaub as a nation was well known to all, but ere these pages come to light it may be forgotten or partially so. A compendium of this history is annexed.

****

The kingdom called the Punjaub extends from the Hindoo Koosh (a branch of the Himalayas) on the north, is bounded by that range on the east, by the Indus to the west, by the Sutlej, to its confluence with the Indus, to the south. However, a considerable portion of the territory *south* of the Sutlej was under the rule of the Lahore Government, and this became the seat of the great war in 1845-6.

This tract of country was consolidated by the conquest of various independent principalities by the ability, enterprise, and foresight of the celebrated Runjeet Singh, who raised himself to pre-eminence and absolute power from the middle class of society. Hence the old Sikh families, the ancient Rajpoots, although subdued into obedience, were ever distrustful of him and he was ever obnoxious to them; hence the seeds of discord which so rapidly sprung up on the decease of Runjeet Singh, and which concluded in this war so fatal to the Sikh.

The whole Punjaub contains about a quarter of a million of Sikhs, the chief part to be found around Lahore and the beautiful city of Umritsir. A Sikh cultivator is seldom seen. The Sikhs, although professing a religion of Brahmanical tenets and established by their great priest and prophet Govind Gooroo, drink to excess, eat opium and *bangh* (a species of wild hemp possessing narcotic and intoxicating qualities of the most enervating description), and regard the abstemious Hindoo and the sensual Mussulman with contempt. Hence the labour of the fields and every other labour fall upon the two latter races, and they have always been favourably disposed to the British.

Runjeet Singh's great policy was a firm adherence to the rulers of British India. He had observed in 1811 the discipline of some of our Seapoys who formed an escort to Mr. Metcalfe (ultimately Lord Metcalfe) on an embassy to the Court of Lahore. This escort, when treacherously attacked by a fanatical sect not then subdued to Runjeet's authority, called Akalies, so boldly and ably defended itself, that, observing the effect of discipline, the acute Runjeet instantly set to work to organize his own army on a similar footing. He invited foreigners, especially Frenchmen, to enter his service, and was liberal to many of them in the extreme. Under such instruction, a most powerful army sprung up, composed of Cuirassiers, Light Infantry most highly equipped, numerous Artillery (in which Runjeet had great faith), and beautifully appointed and organized Infantry. Runjeet spared neither expense nor exertion, and such a spirit of superiority and strength was infused into this army that it believed itself invincible and the most powerful in the world. Runjeet died in June, 1839, leaving this powerful army, estimated by us as of the following strength:

> 40,000 Cavalry, regular and irregular, among which a Brigade of Akalies in cuirasses and chain armour, "The Invincibles."
> 120,000 Regular Infantry.
> Innumerable Irregulars—every inhabitant being a soldier.
> 400 pieces of cannon ready to take the field, Runjeet had spared neither pains nor expense to improve the breed of horses, and his efforts were attended with great success.

From the death of Runjeet Singh in 1839 to 1845 a succession of revolutions and murders of Kings and Princes continued, first one party, then another, supporting a reputed son of Runjeet on the throne, who was as sure to be murdered in the sanguinary struggles of that Reign of Terror. A Hill family, elevated for their personal beauty rather than their talents (although some of them were far from wanting abilities), became conspicuous, and many fell with the puppets of their creation. This family received the soubriquet of Lords of the Hills, Jummoo being the fortified hold of the head of the family. Its most conspicuous members were Goolab Singh and Dhyan Singh. Dhyan and his son Heera Singh were both Prime Ministers, or Wuzeer, and both were murdered in 1844. Such was the power of the standing army, it acknowledged no other authority, set up Kings and deposed them at pleasure, and at the period of the commencement of the war, a boy (Dhuleep Singh), born of a Hill woman of great ability and reputed the son of old Runjeet, was the nominal King, Lal Singh was Wuzeer, and Tej Singh Commander-in-Chief of this rabble (though highly organized and numerous) army. It must be obvious that such a state of things could not last. The resources of the treasury were rapidly consuming, and with them the only power of the Queen Mother, the Rani or Regent, which consisted in her presents and consequent popularity. All the foreign officers had absconded except one Frenchman, a man of neither note nor talent, and a Spanish Engineer by name Hubon, a low-bred man, but clever, acute, and persevering.

The British Government of India had acknowledged this Regency, and was desirous to retain amicable relationship with the Punjaub, but in the middle of the year 1845, so unruly and clamorous for war was the Sikh army, all negotiations terminated, and a state of uncertainty ensued which made it necessary for British India, without declaring hostility, to place itself on a footing to resist it, should so mad an enterprise ensue.

Meanwhile in 1844 Lord Ellenborough was recalled, and succeeded as Governor-General by Sir Henry Hardinge, a statesman and a soldier of Wellington's, in either capacity celebrated for judgment, ability,

The 31st Foot at the battle of Mudki

and foresight. Upon his very arrival, he saw that a rupture with the Punjaub was sooner or later inevitable, and he drew up an able document on the prospects of British India in such an event, which he submitted to the Directors. Immediately afterwards he commenced moving every possible soldier, and commanded the material of war up to the North-West Frontier, while a large flotilla of boats was built at Bombay for the purpose of bridges, and sent up the Indus and thence into the Sutlej opposite Ferozepore, where they were sunk under the left bank of the river. By these arrangements, dictated by a perfect military knowledge and by that foresight which bears the stamp of prediction, Sir Henry Hardinge, in the autumn of 1845, had in readiness for coming events nine regiments of British Infantry, three regiments of British Cavalry, a most powerful train of Field Artillery (with upwards of 100 field-guns, 6 and 9-pounders, and a powerful battering train in progress), a large force of Regular and Irregular Cavalry, and forty regiments of Native Infantry. The isolated post and fortress of Ferozepore had been reinforced by twenty-four field guns, a regiment of British Infantry, and Cavalry and Native Infantry, until a force of upwards of 7000 men composed a Corps under Major-General Sir John Littler, for the double purpose of defending Ferozepore from insult and watching the *ghauts*, or fords, of the Sutlej. The assembling force was put into Brigades and Divisions, and equipped to take the field either on the initiative or defensive.

In December all negotiations and communications between the Regency and ourselves had ceased at the dictation of the Sikh army, which was clamorous for war with the British, and openly vaunted it would place the Rani and her son upon the Imperial Throne of Delhi, and a correspondence was actually established with that city and the line conducting to it, for the supply of provisions to the Sikh army. This act of treachery on the part of British subjects will show what would be the stability of British rule in India on any other basis than that of military power.

The means of obtaining information on the part of our political officers, as results prove, was defective; nor can any credit attach to Sir John Littler as a watchful outpost officer, when the enemy gradually crossed by boats (not a bridge) an army of 70,000 men of all arms, with an immense train of artillery and overwhelming force of cavalry, with stores enormous, and positively established themselves under the Commanders Tej Singh and Lal Singh, ere our authorities were aware of it, civil or military, fortified a strong position near and embracing the village of Ferozeshuhur, and made a demonstration as of attack in front of Ferozepore. This was in the middle of December. This development and invasion called for, and was met by, the most active and vigorous measures on the part of the Governor-General and Council. Every available regiment was pushed forward without waiting to assemble Divisions and Brigades, although all were in order, and a very able organization was effected, as far as the programme went. The troops made double or forced marches, with the result that the force of cavalry under Brigadier White, the 1st Division under Major-General Sir Harry Smith, and one Brigade of the 2nd Division under Major-General Gilbert, reached Moodkee much fatigued and exhausted on the morning of the eventful 28th December. One of the most able and enterprising movements at this stage of the war was the evacuation of Loodiana, except its fort,

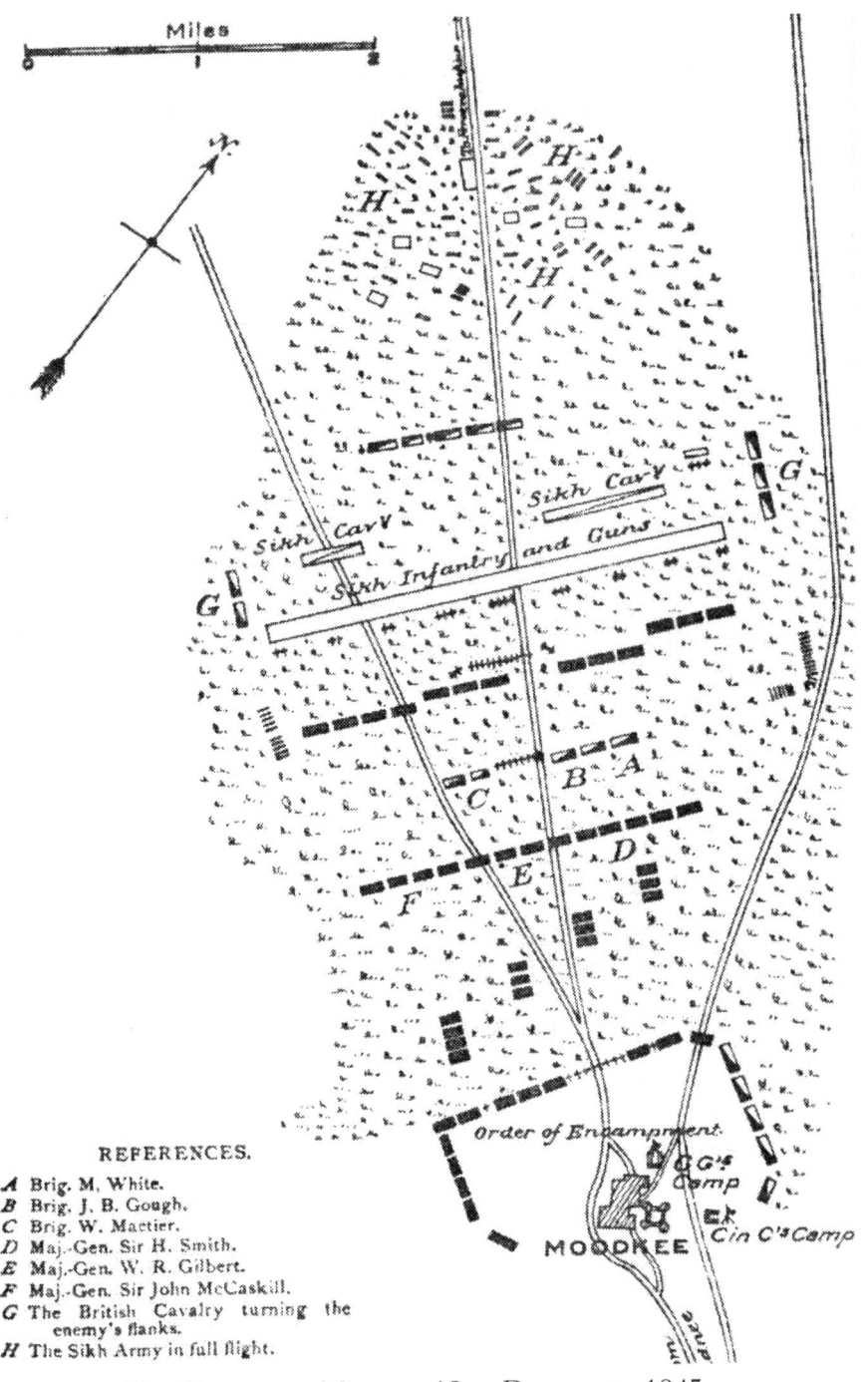

THE BATTLE OF MUDKI—18TH DECEMBER, 1845

by order of the Governor-General, and the march of the troops thence on Busseean, which reinforcement, joining the troops on their hasty march on Moodkee, ensured the victory about to be contended for.

****

Lieutenant-Colonel Burlton on the march to the Battle of Mudki

First comes a bevy of elephants . . . . laden with the tents of European soldiers; then follow long strings of camels, carrying the spare ammunition . . . . and the tents of the native troops. Then again, more camels, carrying hospital stores, wines, medicines, quilts, beds, pots and pans . . . . Imagine a county infirmary, its contents, stock, furniture and stores, to be removed daily some ten or fifteen miles on the backs of camels, and you have some faint idea of this very small portion of our luggage.

Then came *doolies*, or litters. . . . Another long string of camels carrying the day's supply of grain for the cavalry and artillery horses comes next, as well as what are called troop stores—horse clothing, head and heel ropes, pickets, nose bags, spare shoes, etc. The supply of grain for the day for two hundred horses, would need two hundred camels, and for the troop stores as many again. And now comes the private baggage and the tents of the sybarite officers. Finally, the varied groups of women, children, ponies, mules, asses, bullocks and carts laden with all sorts of things . . . .

****

Marching to Mudki, by Private Baldwin, H.M. 9th Regiment of Foot

We hastened towards the Punjaub by forced marches of about 30 miles a-day, along roads of heavy sand, which indeed was hard work for the strongest of us; the marches being so long and fatiguing, and more over, falling short of provisions, in consequence of our camp-followers' inability to keep pace with us, whose cattle, poor things, were nearly harassed out of their lives, and some actually died on the road.

On the 17th, her Majesty's 50th regiment, and some Sepoys from Loodianah, (a station) joined us.

Next morning, (18th) we struck our tents about four o'clock, and moved off; the Artillery and Cavalry were sent on in front in skirmishing order, as the Governor-general and Commander-in-chief had, the previous day, received intelligence from our spies, that the enemy was coming to meet us, we heard the report of guns in front, several times, but no engagement took place.

We marched all, that day, nearly broiled beneath the scorching rays of the sun, and almost choked with clouds of dust, so dense that we could scarcely see each other in the ranks. A few of our men, having weak eyes, had now their sight so impaired by the dust and sand, that they were obliged to go into hospital for medical treatment. Probably you may have heard of the "Acting Corporal," sleeping with one eye open; now I can assure you I have found it a great convenience and comfort at times, marching with one eye open and the other closed, each eye alternately.

You cannot form any idea of what we endured on the march, having nothing to eat or drink until about three o'clock, p.m., when we halted close to a tank of water, where we all got a hearty drink, for which I was as thankful as if the beverage had been so much ale or porter, notwithstanding its being very indifferent water. This tank bore resemblance to a horse-pond in England; in it were elephants, camels, horses, and bullocks; dozens of our *Bheestie-*

wallahs walked in above their knees to procure the clearest of the water for us. When all the troops were supplied with a sufficient quantity, we resumed the march, and reached the camp (Moodkee) in about an hour's time when, to our discomfiture, there was only half a drachm of liquor for each man, being all that had arrived at the camp.

****

On the 18th December a considerable force of the British army had reached Moodkee, much exhausted, as has been said, by the necessary length of marches and a want of water and the power of cooking. Brigades were assembled, but not Divisions. The troops had some of them barely reached their bivouac, when the advance of the Sikh army with clouds of cavalry demanded an immediate turn-out in preparation to resist an attack of fresh and infatuated troops, excited by personal hatred, natural vanity, and the stimulants of spirits, opium, and *bangh*. In place of awaiting the coming storm, our united forces being compact, each arm in support of the other, the whole on an open plain ready to receive the onslaught, our troops were hurried unnecessarily into the field, and the cavalry and artillery rushed into action. Our cavalry and artillery had driven back the Sikh cavalry most gallantly into a very jungly or bushy country, when the enemy's infantry brought them up and occasioned a very considerable and most unnecessary loss. The infantry meanwhile advancing, the right Brigade of the 1st Division upon the right of the army under the command of Brigadier Wheeler, but under the eye of Sir Harry Smith, was fiercely assailed by an almost overwhelming force of Sikh infantry. These it boldly repulsed, and, continuing to advance, took six guns and caused the enemy an inconceivable loss. The dust was so darkening, the enemy could only be discovered by its density and the fire.

The first part of this action was on an open country with occasional large dense and thorny trees, into which the enemy climbed and caused the 50th Regiment great loss. This Brigade (H.M.'s 50th, and the 42nd and 48th Regiments Native Infantry) was more engaged than any other part of the army. Many officers and upwards of 150 soldiers of the 50th were wounded. Brigadier Wheeler was wounded severely; Major-General Sale, Q.M.G. of H.M.'s Forces, who had attached himself to Sir Harry Smith, mortally. On this occasion Sir Harry Smith greatly distinguished himself on his celebrated black Arab "Jim Crow," by seizing one of the colours of H.M.'s 50th Regiment and planting them in the very teeth of a Sikh column, and gloriously did the Regiment rush on with bayonet, and fearful was the massacre which ensued. The left Brigade of the 1st Division was engaged to the left of the line under Brigadier Bolton of H.M.'s 31st Regiment (who fell mortally wounded), while the Brigades of the 2nd Division under Major-General Gilbert and Major-General Sir John McCaskill occupied the centre. Sir John was shot through the heart.

It is a curious circumstance in this battle that so obscured was all vision by the dust, that it afterwards appeared that the bulk of the Sikh forces passed in column along the front of the 1st Brigade of the 1st Division, and when repulsed by the 2nd Brigade 1st Division and 1st Brigade 2nd Division, were driven again across the front of the 50th, the advance of which was pushed by Sir Harry Smith. After the troops were halted, the dust dispelled and the moon was up and shining brightly. The 1st Brigade 1st Division then formed an obtuse angle with the rest of the army. This brigade had gone right through the Sikh repulsed columns. The 1st Division this day took twelve of the seventeen guns captured from the enemy.

****

Lieutenant Robertson of the 31st Foot on the Infantry attack at the Battle of Mudki

We were much broken by the bushes, which would have done well for Light Infantry, but for nothing else, and the men were beginning to get hit. The first person I saw on the ground was Bulkeley, who looked quite dead . . . . I saw a batch of them (sepoys) behind a big tree, firing straight up into the air . . . . The last words I heard Bolton say were, 'Steady 31st, steady, and fire low for your lives!' Cockins, the bugler, was trying to hold the grey horse, when they were all three hit and went down together. This was from the first volley by the enemy. Shortly after Willes was hit, and I took command of No 1 . . . . He said he was hit from behind by the sepoys. Young was hit in the back of the neck, and the buckle of his stock saved him, as the ball came round and out in front. Hart and Brenchley were both hit in the body, and did not live long. We soon get into a regular mob, blazing away at everything in front of us, and nearly as many shots coming from behind us as in front . . . .

I called out to Sir Hugh Gough: 'Where are the guns, and we will soon take them?' and Somerset put his hat on his sword and called out, 'Thirty-first, follow me!' We rushed after him through the smoke, and had the guns in a moment. On we went and came upon two light guns which the enemy were trying to take off the field; but some of our shots hit the horses and brought them to a stand. They then took a shot at us, not twenty yards off; down we went on our noses at the flash, and the grape went over our heads in a shower. I felt it warm; then a rush, and the guns were ours, the gunners not attempting to run away, but cutting at us with their *tulwars*. I think those two guns were taken away by the Sikhs that night, as I never saw them afterwards.

****

PRIVATE BALDWIN, H.M. 9TH REGIMENT OF FOOT,
ON THE INFANTRY AT THE BATTLE AT MUDKI

We flew to arms instantly. There were several men who had taken off their jackets, and had not even time to put them on; and although in a state of exhaustion, we quickly formed parade, and seemed anew invigorated with the prospect of soon being in the midst of battle, which was our darling hope.

It was quite surprising to see with what nimbleness we now repaired to the scene of action, treading over ploughed ground, passing through corn fields, and leaping over numerous small bushes and clumps in our passage; sometimes we had to file in the front and rear, in order to pass the larger thickets.

The enemy were supposed to consist of about 15,000 Infantry, the same force of Cavalry, and 40 guns. They had taken up a position so as to screen themselves behind a thick jungle.

Our small force, about 14,000, including natives, was formed into divisions and brigades, Artillery, Cavalry, and three Infantry divisions.

Cannonading commenced on both sides, sometime ere we (Infantry) could get up. The 5th brigade, consisting of my own corps and two regiments of Sepoys forming part of the 3rd Infantry division, being on the extreme left of the army, were the last engaged. Whilst the other divisions were in action, we took up a position just where the enemy was expected to come. At this time the sable curtain of night had fallen, so that the enemy could not discover the exact strength of our force; and in order that they should not, our division, apart from the others, received orders to lie down, in so doing, we were sheltered from a most tremendous shower of bullets, which whistled over us.

The peculiar sounds of the variety of balls whizzing above our heads, the various distances from us, the faint sounds of our bugles and the enemy's *tumtums*, produced very beautiful music, blended with the noise or thunder of the cannonade, and the musketry of both parties. Being neuter awhile, I could distinguish the different sounds. My position reminded me of a musician in a band, who, when he comes to a part in his music, "tacit," enjoys an opportunity of hearing the harmonious and melodious sounds of such instruments as are playing, but when engaged and his attention, drawn to his own part, he loses the rich melody which floats around him. You cannot form an adequate idea of the splendid music produced by instruments of war when well performed, and we had to play well, otherwise lose the game.

Notwithstanding the Seikhs being most gloriously peppered by the divisions on our right, they neared us who were impatiently waiting to be at them, anxious to mark some with "Britannia." The enemy expected they had had all our force contending with them, and were now endeavouring to get in the rear of our army; had they succeeded, not a man of us could have escaped; being butchered on the field was inevitable.

But when they came near to our line, we up and at them to their surprise and dismay; thus we kept up an incessant fire for some minutes, the barrel of my firelock got so hot that I could hardly bear it in my hand, insomuch as I had to load with the muzzle placed on the cuff of my jacket. We had with us some veterans, who declared they never before heard such splendid file-firing, not even at Waterloo, nor in the Peninsular war. We directed our fire very low, so it did great execution, when, luckily for us, the enemy's bullets came teeming over our heads as thick as hailstones; if we had been mounted on stilts they would have knocked us off, I dare say, for now one of our men had a musket shot pass through the top of his cap, but it did not touch his head; at this time the balls seemed to rend the very atmosphere above us. It appears that our unexpected fire paralyzed the Seikhs, and finding great gaps in their ranks, they retreated in confusion, leaving behind them 17 pieces of brass cannon, I suppose for us to fight them with at some future time.

Now our bugles in every direction sounded the cease-firing, and as soon as the guns left off talking, we cheered, and our cavalry charged; who found that some of the enemy had crept into bushes, and others had climbed up trees, where our men could not get at them with their swords, but resorted to their carbines and shot some of the runagates.

****

STAFF SERGEANT N. W. BANCROFT OF THE BENGAL
HORSE ARTILLERY ON CASUALTIES AT
THE BATTLE OF MUDKI

We sustained many casualties in this purely artillery duel, and there were many narrow escapes. There were some terrible sights to be seen; and the writer saw one in particular which he will never forget. A ventsman of one of our guns was actually running about disembowelled; the powder-pouch worn on his side had been struck by a shell and exploded. Some of the escapes were absolutely miraculous. A corporal had the port-fire in his hand shattered with a round shot while he was in the act of firing his gun, and he had also to be reprimanded for the language he used on the occasion. It may here be added, that this very non-commissioned officer had to be helped in and out of the saddle from weakness, the result of a long and painful illness: he subsequently died from exhaustion..

The present writer had rather a close shave himself on the occasion—the horse he was riding appeared very uneasy about the head, and at the same instant he himself felt a very peculiar sensation in his own right ear, on stooping forward to examine the horse's head he found its right ear split. The rear-rank man had trained this horse, and the writer turned in his saddle to inform him of his favourite's misfortune. The man was leaning over his holsters at the front of the saddle, as if resting himself. On attempting to rouse him, he literally sprang out of the saddle, fell to the ground and rolled over, face uppermost; a ball had passed through the horse's right ear, and passing by the writer's right ear, penetrated his comrade's right eye. Its direction was perfectly straight.

On looking back to our wagon train, the writer saw that another of his comrades had fallen; he, too, had been shot through the right eye: looking to his left, he saw a gunner, an old friend of his, sitting up in his saddle after a round shot had passed through his breast; he had to be lifted out of his saddle, put into a *doolie*, and carried to the rear. These sights, were

The the 3rd Light Dragoons at Mudki

not the most pleasant, and were calculated to make a young soldier rather squeamish than otherwise, but the disagreeable feeling soon wore away.

This desperate game continued to be played for sometime, when the two nine-pounder batteries came up, one on each flank, and we had now 42 guns in full play. These the Sikhs evidently found too many for them, for their fire sensibly slackened, and we received orders to "cease firing," but owing to the excited state of the men, Bully Brookes, our Brigadier, found no small difficulty in having his order obeyed; and it must be confessed that a few more rounds were given on our own account, before limbering up. Just then our cavalry came to the front, under Brigadiers Gough and White, and executed some brilliant manoeuvres. They soon put the enemy's cavalry to flight, and silenced their guns, but only for a time.

****

THE BATTLE OF MUDKI AS RECALLED BY LIEUTENANT GEORGE DENHAM-COOKES OF THE 3RD LIGHT DRAGOONS

We watered & picketed our Horses, & our Messman having by some luck laid hold of a little grub, which we stood much in need of, having had scarcely anything to eat for the previous 6 days, we got under a tree and commenced operations. We had made a little progress when a Native Trooper came up to us as hard as he could lick, & just managed to stammer out 'Seik', 'Seik'. At the same time the Infantry bugles and drums sounded a beat to arms. We luckily had not unsaddled, and were formed in close column in 5 minutes ....

By this time the Enemy's guns had opened .... The Comdr. in Chief then ordered us to attack the Enemy's left flank, which was fast surrounding our camp.

We advanced in open column of troops, the Comdr. in Chief & his staff taking off their cocked hats & cheering us. This was a fine inspiring sight, but it did a great deal of mischief, as it maddened our men & prevented the officers from keeping them back . . . .

We kept advancing at a gallop—the dust was so thick that I could not see my horse's head, but every now & then I felt him bound into the air & found that he had jumped a bush.

The enemy had now discovered us & the round shot came tearing thro' our ranks. The first shot took off a Trumpeter's head just behind me . . . .

Our pace now increased, & the leading Troops (the only ones who could see their way as they had no dust) came upon the Enemy. From that moment, owing to thick dust & the quantities of bushes and trees, the Regt. was dispersed.

I went on by myself, my Troop having gone, I know not whither, & the first object I saw was an Akali who let fly & missed me. I then came on two more rascals, who did the same, one of whom tasted my sabre, which I found would not cut thro' him, as he was enveloped in cotton clothes. ... I soon after found a couple of my own men, & at the same time an Elephant came by us, with 4 Seik Chiefs making the best of their way off. If I had had a few more men I could have taken them.

At this time I was in rear of the Enemy, & having gone far enough I turned back & met Hale, Fisher, Swinton (who was wounded) & a few Dragoons. About this time we met two Seiks under a tree, & Martin of the Native Cavalry attacked one of them, but in so stupid a way that the Seik sent his spear clean through Martin's breast & out at his back . . . . I saw it was no use attacking these rascals with a sword, so I bethought me of my pistol; the right barrel missed fire, but the left did its duty well, & doubled the rascal up. Hale shot the other fellow.

We continued on our return, when we came on a body of about 3,000 Seik Cavalry behind a Village, directly on our road home. We saw there was nothing for it but to cut our way through. The Native Cavalry with us would not come on; but we went at them, as hard as we could go. Then the Seiks opened right & left, & gave us a most infernal volley—wounded Fisher, & killed 3 Dragoons ....

After we had dispersed the rascals in the charge, those that were not cut down took to the Trees and Bushes, where we could not reach them, & from this secure position they shot a number of our men .... After a short time we got our Carbines out & brought down 7 rascals out of one Tree, so they did not have it all their own way....

At daybreak next morning, I escorted Sir Hugh Gough over the field of battle. The Commander-in-Chief halted when we came to the village where we had fought the previous evening, and ordered us to go in & cut down every man we could find, as the Sikhs had 'used our men most cruelly'.

One of my brother officers, a remarkably fine fellow, was found 'with his throat cut from ear to ear; two musket balls through him, & two arrows sticking in him, & several sabre cuts; in fact, all our dead had been frightfully disfigured—all had their throats cut, and several were beheaded. I might have killed several Seiks at Moodkee; but it being my first battle, I was foolishly merciful ....

****

Sir Harry Smith's Division lost at Moodkee: 79 killed, 339 wounded and 19 missing. Both Brigadiers were knocked down, and one died of his wounds. After the action the troops returned to their camp, which they reached about half-past twelve.

Early in the morning of the 19th parties were sent out to bring in the wounded, and our cavalry outposts pushed forward to cover this, as also to enable our artillery to bring in the captured guns, amounting to seventeen. The enemy having made a reconnaissance with a large body of cavalry, which created an alarm in the camp, the troops were turned out and took up a very faulty position in front of Moodkee. In this village there is a very tenable little fort, which was of great use to us. About one o'clock, the enemy making no forward movement, the troops were turned in to cook. During the afternoon all was quiet.

CHAPTER 5

The Battle of Ferozeshah

FROM HARRY SMITH'S AUTOBIOGRAPHY

On the 20th every arrangement was made for the care of the sick, wounded, stores, etc., at Moodkee, and the troops, well completed in ammunition, prepared to march on the memorable 21st December. As yet no direct communication was established with Sir John Littler, in command of the 7000 men at Ferozepore. These were still isolated and subject to a weighty attack of the enemy, who could attack with facility and still hold his position around the village of Ferozeshuhur. This was strongly fortified and bristling with cannon, and there was plenty of water for both men and horses. Hence our object was to effect a combination with the Ferozepore force ere the enemy anticipated us, unless his correct information of our movements led him to attack either one or both of our columns moving mutually to a point of concentration, for Littler's force was ordered to move out and meet our advance. (This was by no means a difficult or dangerous movement, the distance from Moodkee to Ferozepore not exceeding that from the Sikh army at Ferozeshuhur.)

The troops marched from Moodkee in order of battle (almost crossing the front of the enemy's position), and moved in the direction of Ferozepore, from whence Littler's column was also moving to effect the junction, which took place about ten o'clock in the morning. Sir H. Hardinge, as Governor-General, had interdicted any attack upon the enemy's lines until the junction was effected, a most fortunate interdiction for British India. So soon as the army was collected, Sir H. Hardinge turned to Sir H. Gough and said, "Now the army is at your disposal."

Sir Hugh made immediate arrangements to attack, although much most valuable time was lost in those arrangements, nor were Generals of Division made the least aware of how or what or where they were to attack. The army was one unwieldy battalion under one Commanding Officer who had not been granted the power of ubiquity. My opinion may be called one after the result, but I formed it while the troops were arranging in order of battle. I now record it leisurely and most deliberately. Had I commanded, I should have moved in contiguous columns of brigades, my cavalry protecting my advance up to the enemy's position till within range of his guns, the troops so moving as to be able to anticipate any movement of the enemy to the discomfort of Ferozepore, and to enable me to throw the weight of the attack upon the right of the enemy, if, as I apprehended from all I had heard, he was as assailable upon his right as on any other given point.

I say I would have thrown the weight of my attack upon his right, because he was most formidable in his entrenched position, and if that right was to be carried as I anticipated, my victorious troops could have acted on the line of his retreat, which, being comparatively left open, gave him an opportunity to avail himself of it, and not to fight with that desperation that even bad troops will show if they are hemmed in.

So soon as my advancing columns had attained to barely within the range of the enemy's guns, I would have carefully

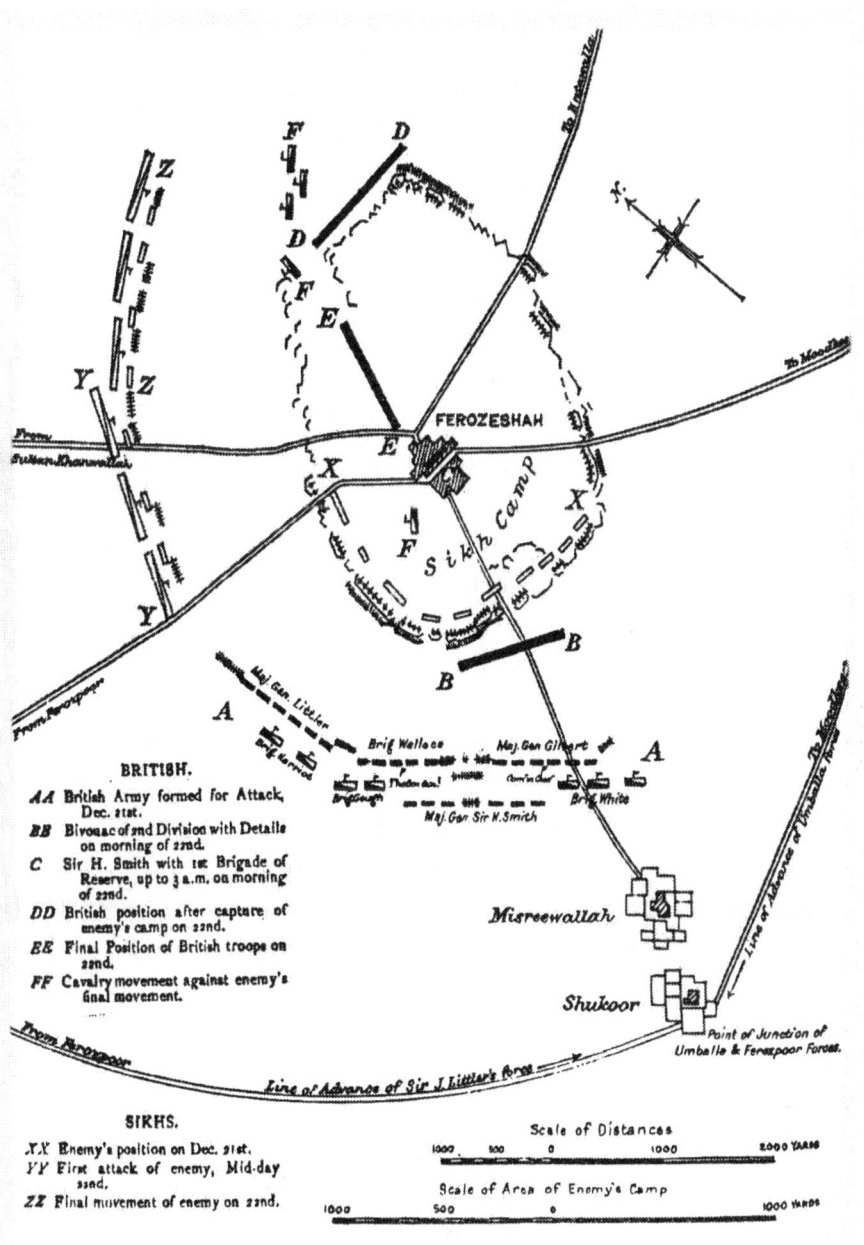

THE BATTLE OF FEROZESHAH—21ST DECEMBER, 1845

reconnoitred him, and compared ocular demonstration with the accounts of the enemy's interior arrangements of defence afforded by spies, taking with me each General of Division as I passed the front of his troops. This reconnaissance would have enabled officers in command to see their way.

The whole weight of my attack should have been on the enemy's right and right centre, which would have given me the advantage which the principles of war so justly and truly demand, "To be superior to your enemy on the point of attack." The enemy's position was his favoured one, semicircular, the centre near the village of Ferozeshuhur, where there were good wells, and also pond water for cattle. By a weighty attack on a given point, the half of the enemy's cannon in position would have been lost to him and innocuous to us. Whereas we attacked in what may almost be termed lines of circumvallation of the enemy's crescent, thus presenting ourselves as targets to every gun the enemy had.

Our artillery was massed about the centre of the army; six-pounders opposed to the enemy's guns in embrasures, and of a calibre or weight beyond the range of our six-pounders; hence the mortality and wrongly imputed inefficiency of that arm, a noble arm when called forth in its legitimate field.

The 1st Division, mine, was separated, the 1st Brigade, under Brigadier Hicks, being to the right of the mass of artillery, the 2nd Brigade to the left of that arm, which covered from three-quarters to a mile of ground. The whole Division was regarded as the reserve to the centre of the army. Sir John Littler's, the Ferozepore force, was on the left. In this order the army advanced to the attack. There was plenty of daylight; the imputation of attacking too late in the day is unfounded, as I will plainly show, although I was not then, nor am I now, an advocate for so precipitate an attack, made without any knowledge of the enemy's position beyond the lies and contradictory stories of spies. An attack on a rear-guard ought to be precipitated *coûte que coûte*; an attack on an army delayed until science can be applied with the greatest decision.

Having posted my right Brigade, I joined the left and correctly posted it, strictly in obedience to the orders I had received from the Commander-in-Chief in person. My Division thus posted, I rode forward with a desire of having a look at the enemy's position, and came up to Sir H. Hardinge, who was in doubt what some guns were upon our left, which had just been brought into action. I galloped forward to ascertain, and reported they were of Littler's force, that his attack appeared to me one of no weight from its formation, and that, if the enemy behaved as expected, it would fail. Sir H. Hardinge said, "Then bring up your Division." I explained I had only one Brigade; I could bring up that. He ordered it up, and I pretty quickly had it on the move to the front, to the left of Gilbert's, or the 2nd Division, and to the right of Littler's.

****

PRIVATE BALDWIN, H.M. 9TH REGIMENT OF FOOT,
ON THE INFANTRY BATTLE AT FEROZESHAH

Our brigade formed the reserve of the left division, and met with some monstrous sharp work, as you will perceive. Cannonading commenced with both parties, nearly an hour before the Infantry had a chance of using their shooting sticks. The 62nd regiment's brigade formed the advance of the left division, and were the first to charge an immense battery of guns, and of heavy battering calibre, which had opened a fierce fire upon us. Meantime our brigade advanced to within range of the enemy's long shots, which came rolling down upon us, though with half-spent velocity, and being very large we could perceive them as they bounded along, in time to open out, and let them pass through our ranks.

We were greatly annoyed here by the bushes, as we were at Moodkee. I think verily these Seikhs must bear some affinity to the "bush rangers" in New Zealand, from their choosing these blackguard places to fight in.

As we neared the camp their shots became dangerous, making a few gaps in our line, and, when arriving at where the balls came with greater force, we were ordered to lie down, which we did flat as pancakes! as you may readily guess. In this position we remained a short time, the balls bounding over by hundreds, but not injuring us in the least. But soon, however, our bugles sounded the "arise," then we rose and advanced a little nearer to the scene of action, when the balls came whish! whish! whish! over us in all directions, and I regret to say severed the heads, legs, and wings of some of our poor unfortunate fellows.

Again we were ordered to lie down, to which you may suppose we felt no objection. Our position at the time reminded me of being caught in a very heavy tempest some distance from home, and finding a place of shelter on the spot, keeping there till the storm abated, and afterwards proceeding home dry and comfortable. And so we were in hopes the enemy would diminish their fire upon us ere long, that we might advance nearer without incurring such risk as the present circumstances foreboded. But if we had been sheltered there till this time, to all appearances their fire would have been as furious as ever. While in that position we laid listening to the apparent desperate work with the advance bri-

The 62nd Regiment at the Battle of Ferozeshah

gade, then assailing the tremendous battery in front of us an incessant fire was kept up for sometime by our people, but hearing a cessation we surmised that the 62nd were sick of shooting and had had recourse to their bayonets; shortly afterwards, seeing them return so orderly and deliberately as they did, we thought they had carried the battery, and that others were then directed toward us.

I began to fear that I should not have any sport whatever, but had come on a "wild-goose chase." But I afterwards found the aspect of things much darker than I had conjectured, for the men of the 62nd were cut down by dozens at the bores of the cannon; the survivors, poor fellows, after cutting and pelting away for some minutes witnessing numbers of their comrades falling around, were obliged to retire burning with revenge; as they passed by our right flank, they gave us to understand there were "breakers ahead" which indeed was true enough, for when our squadron sailed up to them, it was in a measure wrecked.

Our General having been killed at Moodkee, Brigadier Wallace was appointed to command our brigade, who was killed shortly after giving us the word "charge;" and as we were doubling towards the volcanic battery which made such fearful devastation amongst the 62nd regiment, our Colonel's horse was shot from under him, but he, nothing daunted, led us on foot, sword in hand. He (Colonel Taylor) was well known to be as brave officer, and, I regret to say, fell a victim in this memorable charge.

Two days after we found his lifeless body lying on the field, clasped in the arms of a soldier of my company; from the position in which the two dead bodies laid, we conjectured that, the former was wounded, in the first instance, and the latter was in the act of carrying him to the rear, when a shower of grape shot killed them both.

There were also nearly twenty others of our regiment lying round, them; several of whom had been cut and mutilated in a most frightful manner by the treacherous foe during the night. Coming to the, point, is a favourite maxim, and I can now say, that for once in my life I have been obliged, to come to the point, and that too of the sword and bayonet.

Our loss in the charge was considerable, especially in the left wing of the regiment, consisting of my company, three others and part of another; the greater part of the right wing happily escaped the tremendous fire from this terrific battery, and the mournful result of storming, being detached from us, and engaged in setting fire to the, enemy's camp, and exploding some of their magazines; scores of poor fellows, were cut down by discharges from this prodigious battery, in the same manner as the richest flower (wheat) in England falls from the scythe.

The Seikh Artillery, with whom we contended, were picked men, both for valour and size ; they were indeed gigantic, their usual stature being from six feet to six feet three inches, muscular and active in proportion. We were only like Lilliputians in comparison with those huge monsters, and I marvel they did not kill us all and swallow us slick out of the way. Had they been without tasting food for awhile, I am sure we should have been but a scanty meal for their numerous army, but fortunately they had been well fed, or possibly we might have become their prey. Yet I do not wish you to think them cannibals; on the contrary, respecting their diet, they are inclined to fastidiousness, never eating beef or pork, nor does any Indian eat pork excepting ham, which is exported from England, and he evades the law by calling it "European mutton." Playing thus given you a slight description of the Seikhs' position, you will observe it was not eating but fighting with us.

We lost lots of men before we got to the enemy's principal battery, for we were pushed, as it were, into the lion's mouth; when we did reach it the gunners resorted to their *tol-wols* and we our bayonets, then came the "tug of war"—with clashing of steel in earnest.

In describing, to the best of my ability, the most desperate conflict which then took place, I might present to your imagination such scenes of horror as were never before witnessed in this country, although the Indians are for ever at war, either with the British or among themselves.

What a picture of horror I beheld when we and the Seikhs were straining every nerve to deeds of barbarity, wholly bent on mutual destruction, wielding sanguinary weapons, swords, and bayonets.

The ground in a few minutes was sprinkled with the blood of hundreds of brave men. With what anguish of heart I heard the moanings of the wounded and the shrieks of the dying, yet, at such time, compassion is swallowed up in the wild uproar of fierce passion and deadly animosity.

Those overgrown brutes of artillery men had great advantage over us, and they fought with unusual courage, many of their lives being bought at the price of ours, i.e, when some of our men plunged their bayonets into the Seikhs, they held them fast by the sockets with their left hands, and cut our men's heads off with their massive tol-wols; with deep regret I saw several of my comrades thus killed, and in my first exploit with the bayonet I was within a day's march of sharing the same fate, but, providentially, I had the presence of mind to relinquish the left hand grasp of my musket as soon as the bayonet had penetrated the body of my antagonist, who, as I expected, made a dexterous cut at me, but with no effect. I extricated my bayonet instantly, when he fell, muttering something which I could not understand, and soon expired. I did not stay to close his eyes, but kept the game alive with my then tried taw, not a marble one, but a steel one.

Till now I was unconscious of having spilt the blood of any of the enemy, though I fired at them times enough, both at Moodkee, and on the present occasion, ere we came to close quarters, to annihilate; a whole' battalion, provided my exertions had been successful. I shall for ever entertain a most lively recollection of that not "cricket match" but "*skivering* match."

Here I absolutely saw the dead, as it were, killing the living. This may seem incredible to you, but. to be more explicit: when a man of ours succeeded in burying his bayonet in the Seikh's body he considered him hors-de-combat, but the enemy, (in his dying agonies, and determined to sell his life as dearly as possible,) grasping the bayonet with the left hand and mustering a last effort, generally succeeded in dealing such a blow with, his tol-wol from the right-hand, as to lay his assailant prostrate, and thus both fell mortally wounded in the fearful struggle. Just at the time we had butchered all the gunners of the battery, cries of "Cavalry coming" rang in our ears; we were then in a very awkward situation, higgledy-piggledy, helter-skelter among the guns; after having therefore spiked a few of them, we withdrew to a more open spot, where we might better defend ourselves against any sudden attack.

Here we were destitute of a commander, till the only surviving captain of our regiment, who, by the bye, was severely wounded in the arm, (a son of the Rev. Borton, of Blofield, Norfolk,) took the command, and ordered us to form square and resist, cavalry, at the same time exclaiming, "your colours, men! for God's sake, men, guard your colours !" which, I believe, we were resolved to. do to a man, without such marked injunction from our new commander.

At this time night came on, and the enemy's Cavalry had not the courage to come up for fear of being taken by surprise in the dark. We remained for some time in square, but finding the Cavalry were not forthcoming we, retired, formed companies, and numbered off by files, sections, and sub-divisions; our whole line numbered 110 files, which made 220 men, out of about 800, prior to the charge; the others, not being present, we thought were either killed or wounded, knowing that full 250 must have fallen at the battery with us.

Shortly afterwards an aide-de-camp came, who inquired what regiment we were? Being told the remains of the 9th, he informed us that he had just left 300 or thereabouts of our men in a part of the enemy's camp which cheered us not a little. In this position, we continued till further orders, beholding the Seikhs' camp in a blaze, which presented a most striking and sublime spectacle; torrents of fire illuminated the horizon to a great distance, the stars in the heavens seemed eclipsed, and repeated explosions of powder mines, rendered the scene awful beyond description.

The Seikhs' entrenched camp was about a mile in length, and half a mile in breadth, including within its area the village of Ferozeshuhur, with upwards of 100 guns, half of them of heavy battering calibre, dispersed over their position, which was entrenched and defended by European skill. The enemy's cannonade made great ravages throughout our force; our Artillery being unable to silence theirs, and our Cavalry force very weak, although the 3rd Dragoons did wonders., but the great weight of the battle fell upon us, (Infantry) and we had succeeded in carrying a part of the Seikhs' entrenchments before retiring to wile away the night.

The aide-de-camp who so recently left us went back to our other men, telling them of our safety; three of whom (grenadiers) soon found their way to us, stating that the right wing had been, and were then, setting fire to the Seikhs' camp, exploding magazines, and had sustained scarcely any loss. These men were as pleased to see us as we were them, for they had great fear of our being killed, and the colours of the regiment lost, which were with us.

****

LIEUTENANT JOHN CUMMING OF THE 80TH FOOT
ON THE INFANTRY ATTACK AT THE
BATTLE OF FEROZESHAH

We advanced against a hailstorm of round-shot, shells, grape and musketry. To heighten the destruction mines had been dug before the trenches and sprung under our feet: the slaughter was terrible. Yet our fellows pressed nobly on with the charge, and with the bayonet alone rushed over the entrenchments and captured the guns in front of us. The Sikhs flinched not an inch, but fought till they died to a man at their guns. Our further advance was checked by the bursting mines setting their camp on fire, and we retired a short distance to be clear of it.

Sir Hugh Gough

****

Private Baldwin, H.M. 9th Regiment of Foot, on the cavalry charge at Ferozeshah

Sir Hugh Gough finding we were unable to beat the enemy back, ingeniously devised a plan formidable enough to frighten them; his stratagem was, placing all our Cavalry force behind the bushes, some distance off the camp. Being thus arranged, they extended about two miles. I must tell you the, bushes in this locality are almost as intricate as a maze. The battle at this crisis was decidedly in favour of the Seikhs, and as our last resource, the bugles sounded the "charge," when instantly all our Cavalry rushed out from their position, and being thus extended, there appeared to be thousands of them; and from the dense cloud of dust they occasioned, the enemy could not discover their weakness. Our having expected daily the arrival of the 9th and 16th Lancers, and seeing apparently such a strong force of horsemen, and unconscious at the time of the shrewd scheme of Sir Hugh's, the general cry throughout our Infantry was, that the 9th and 16th were come at last. "Look at them boys! there they go as fresh as daisies." We were all transported with ecstasy at the idea of their coming so timely. The officers brandished their swords, and we soldiers waved our bayonets and shouted from the top of our voices, "On, on to the charge ye brave! ye brave!" &c.

We Infantry prepared to resist the enemy's Cavalry, in case ours should be repulsed, but happily they were not; on the contrary, they routed the enemy, and took possession of all their guns and ammunition, making 91 captured in this battle.

We were surprised, and really amused, when the Cavalry returned from the charge, at finding they were only the 3rd Dragoons and native Cavalry, whose loss, you may guess, was considerable.

****

The Battle of Ferozeshah as recalled by Lieutenant George Denham-Cookes of the 3rd Light Dragoons

Old White sent me to see where the Cavalry were going to. I galloped to the rear, and as I was going a round shot came behind me, & struck within a foot of my horse's legs: he almost fell down from fright.

On reaching the Cavalry, I gave old White's message, and they said, 'We have orders to go to Ferozepore, and have a man to shew us the way; you had better come also.'

I replied, 'I will see you —— first!'

I regret to say that some of our men shirked off, & also 2 or 3 officers, whom I have cut in consequence. It was indeed a fearful time.

On my return I gave my answer to old White, & at the same moment an A.D.C. came down & said that the Enemy's Cavalry were about to attack . . . . I regret to say that some of our men fell out, I hope because their horses could not move. We had not more than 74 men left. Old White disappeared & so did Sullivan (a regular cur). Old Hale and I cheered on our men, & I never was more relieved than when an A.D.C. came & told us that the enemy were in full retreat!! and that we were only to press them. We did so: it is lucky that we had no more to do—it seemed like an interposition of Providence, the Enemy's retreating at this time, when they had only to advance to win the battle . . . .

****

Staff Sergeant N. W. Bancroft of the Bengal Horse Artillery on the action at the Battle of Ferozeshah

The advance was again sounded, and we had not proceeded far when we fell in with Littler's force, consisting of 5,500 men and 21 guns, which had pushed on from Ferozepore to join the Commander-in-Chief. We were again halted as the heat was intense, the dust sharp and thick, and water very scanty, hut nevertheless, the time passed pleasantly enough, for we were engaged in looking up *shipmates* (i.e., men who had come to India in the ship) and *townies* (fellow townsmen), in the force that had joined us.

It was in the midst of these recognitions and greetings that we heard the first shot from the enemy, but in an instant every man was in his place, and the different columns moved off to their allotted positions. We were in the left column under Sir Henry Hardinge. Our route now lay through a dense jungle, and on emerging from which we found ourselves upon a level plain, and exposed to a most murderous artillery fire. Indeed, so hot was it, that an infantry regiment, the "9th Holy Boys," covering our guns, was ordered to lie down, not, however, before wide gaps had been made in their ranks by chain-shot. It is believed their Colonel was among the number killed.

At this juncture an A.-D.-C. rode up with instructions for the horse artillery to gallop to the front and open fire, which was done. Here the writer's comrade's horse was killed by a cannon shot through the body, which left him with one leading horse. The A.-D.-C. who brought the order never returned to his chief. A second A.-D.-C. soon galloped up with orders to approach yet more closely to the enemy's batteries; this second A.-D.-C. met the same fate as the first, for both their horses were seen running wild about the field without their riders.

It being found that our light six-pounder guns produced but slight effect on the enemy's heavier metal, before carrying out the last order, our major, evidently with the object of ascertaining how close it would be necessary for him to advance, laid one of the guns himself, ordering it to be fired; he stepped aside to note the result, which must have disappointed him, as he was observed to stamp his foot impatiently. He turned round in search of his horse and not seeing it, he said—his last words, alas?—"Bancroft, where is my horse?"

Pointing to the direction in which the animal was standing, the writer answered: "There he is, Sir!"

The words were scarcely uttered, when he saw the gallant major lying at a little distance from his horse—headless! The shot must have struck him full in the face, for there was no trace or vestige of his features to be seen. At the same moment the writer felt a dreadful shock on his right side, and his right arm involuntarily whirled round his head (it was the same cannon shot which killed our major.) He was at -the time picking out a quid of tobacco from a comrade's pouch to moisten his lips withal. Feeling that he was hit, he returned the pouch, with the left hand, remarking—"Here, take your pouch, I have lost my arm!" The shot had passed between his body and right arm, carrying away his pouch and belt on the one side, and the soft parts of the arm itself on the other.

Being disabled, he was told to dismount and make room for a better man. He dismounted and planted himself at the butt of a tree within the line of guns.

The troop was now about to change its position, but as the writer did not see the force of being left on the field, he immediately betook himself to a seat on one of the limber-boxes, and beside him was placed the headless body of the poor major.

The effect of the wound the writer had received now began to be felt; the loss of blood increased his thirst, but there was no water to be had, and the sight of the headless body certainly made his position anything but enviable, and he was compelled to relinquish his seat and look out for another. It was fortunate for him he did so; a second cannon shot severed the body he had just left in halves! Some of the gunners observing this, picked up the shattered remains, tied them up in a horse-blanket, and refastened them on the same box.

It was now getting dusk; the troop was in a frightfully crippled state from the loss it had sustained in men and horses, there being only a young lieutenant (W. A. Mackinnon) in charge. Still the troop advanced, and in the advance the writer took his seat on the trail of a wagon, and felt for a short time pretty comfortable. But only for a very short time: the gun on his right halted in consequence of its two polemen being literally cut in two, the lower portions of their bodies still remaining in the saddle, the upper portion of the right pole-man's body being on the ground, while that of the left was suspended by the head over the collar-bar.

The sergeant-major brought up a spare man to take the place of the near pole-man, at the same time emptying the two saddles of their ghastly burdens. It must be said that the spare man hesitated to jump into the saddle—for one of the mangled bodies was that of his brother! The sergeant-major seeing there was no time to be lost, freed the collar-bar from the half body hanging over it, and threatened the spare gunner with his pistol if he did not jump into the saddle immediately, and he did so.

The gun on the writer's left had now halted; the off pole-man having been struck by a round shot in the face, which carried away the left half, the body still sitting erect in the saddle. Here another spare man ran up, tilted the body out of the saddle, and sprang up into his seat, which he had scarcely attained when a shot broke the off fore-leg of the horse he had just mounted. The horse was sent adrift, but appeared loath to leave his mates on the advance of the battery, for he hobbled after it, and as ill-luck would have it, came blundering up to the wagon, on the beam of which the writer was seated, and poked himself between the wheels of the limber and wagon, putting an end to all progress for a time. Holding on with his left arm, the writer tried his utmost to keep the brute off with his feet; but a cannon ball soon solved the difficulty. It struck the horse on the hind quarter, causing him to bound forward, and knock the writer off his perch, placing him in imminent danger of being run over.

There is one incident which may be worth relating here: prior to his being knocked off his seat, a ball struck the pole horse of the wagon on which the writer was seated, in the stomach, and in an instant the poor animal's intestines were hanging about its leg. The writer called to the rider informing him of the mishap in language more plain than refined perhaps by saying "Tom! Tom!" (the man's name was Tom Connolly) "Snarly Yow (the horse's name) has turned inside out, and his *inwards* are dangling about!"

The Bengal Native Army

Tom shouted to the corporal leading the team, "Joe! Joe! Pull up! Snarly's g—ts are hanging about his legs!"

To which request the corporal coolly made answer: "Begorra, Tom, I would'nt pull up at such a time as this if you're own g—ts were hanging out!"

The writer was afterwards told that the horse did not drop until the troop formed battery again at a considerable distance to the right.

The enemy's cavalry could be seen hanging about at no great distance so it was hopeless for him to attempt to procure another seat, the troop having broken into a gallop to avoid the enemy's cavalry charging them, so he was left behind to himself among his dead comrades, and being in great pain, and much in need of rest, he was fain to lay himself down by the side of the dead horse which had caused his second mishap, and screen himself, the best way he could, from the view of the enemy's cavalry; for they showed no mercy to the wounded.

He must have remained here till about midnight, when he was considerably astonished at hearing, no great distance off, the voices of Europeans. He gladly hailed them, and found them to be wounded infantrymen on their way to the rear—if they could find it. As a matter of course, the writer joined them, but as none of them had the slightest idea of their whereabouts; or where they were wandering (for it was pitch dark) they made up their minds to halt under the first tree they came across. They found one shortly, and made another discovery, namely, that they were not out of the range of the enemy's fire, for the tree was struck several times during their stay under it.

They were not, however, very long here when they heard the rumbling sound of wheels, and remained perfectly silent to discover, if possible, whether those advancing were friends or foes. Happily they proved the former; it was Horsford's 9-pounder battery, which had marched out with us from Umballa.

Here the writer met with old friends, who had known him when he was a boy serving with them in the same battalion of foot artillery—"The Fighting 4th." Several of his companions were found dead under the tree which had sheltered them; they had died from sheer loss of blood and want of water. Such of them as were alive were accommodated on the wagons, and taken on to the main body of the artillery headquarters, from whence the recall was sounded by order of Brigadier Brookes, in order, if possible to assemble all the artillery together for the night.

Here were found all the troops of horse artillery, with the exception of the writer's own; being questioned about the troop's whereabouts, he could only answer up to the time he had left it—or rather, it had left him. There was a well here, which was surrounded by hundreds of thirsty souls, all patiently waiting their turn for a drink, the writer's share consisting of a handful of mud, from which he in vain endeavoured to extract some moisture. The mud he placed into his wound, which seemed to stanch the bleeding somewhat, and then laid himself down on the softest bit of earth he could find with his head between the spokes of a gun wheel for a pillow and tried to get a little sleep. This, however, was impossible, in consequence of the pain of the wound and the severity of the cold till day-break.

He ascertained, subsequently, that his troop had, during the night, strayed away under the enemy's entrenchments, so close as to be within pistol shot, which, of course, prevented them from replying to the bugles which had been sounded during the night to recall it. Meanwhile, it was generally reported among the other troops of horse artillery, that the "second of the first" had been cut up to a man.

At day-break on the 22nd, the troop was discovered, simultaneously by us and by the enemy, who immediately opened fire on it. They were unable to return the enemy's fire, their ammunition being quite exhausted, and the horses, jaded and fagged beyond measure; the second set of horses with the six spare ammunition wagons (well stocked), drawn by bullocks, could not be found in the night. The troop was rescued from its more than perilous position by the despatch of another troop of horse artillery to its relief, and strange to say the enemy's fire had no effect on either of our batteries. The only way in which this bad practice of the enemy can be accounted for is, that during the night their heavy guns were in an entrenched camp, and they kept up their fire all night. They, perhaps, never thought of running up their guns after each discharge, but allowed the trails to sink lower into the earth, which caused too great an elevation of the gun's muzzles to produce any effect on our guns, though they were quite within range of the enemy's fire.

****

MAJOR W. S. R. HODSON OF THE
1ST BENGAL EUROPEAN FUSILIERS ON
THE BATTLE OF FEROZESHAH

Our Sepoys could not be got to face the tremendous fire of the Sikh artillery, and as usual, the more they quailed the more the English officers exposed themselves in vain efforts to bring them on . . . . At Ferozeshah on the evening of the 21st, as we rushed towards the guns in the most dense dust and smoke, and under an unprecedented fire of grape, our Sepoys again gave way and broke. It was a fearful crisis, but the bravery of the English regiments saved us. A ball struck my leg below the knee, but happily spared the bone. I was also knocked down twice, once by a shell bursting so close to me as to kill the men behind me, and once by the explosion of a magazine. The wound in my leg is nothing, as you may judge when I tell you that I was on foot or horseback the whole of the two following days.... No efforts could bring the Sepoys forward, or half the loss might have been spared, had they rushed on with the bayonet.... Just as we were going into action, I stumbled on poor Carey, whom you may remember. On going over the field on the 30th, I found the body actually cut to pieces by the keen swords of the Sikhs, and but for his clothes could not have recognized him. I had him carried into camp for burial, poor fellow, extremely shocked at the sudden termination of our renewed acquaintance.... I enjoyed all, and entered into it with great zest, till we came to actual blows, or rather, I am (now) half ashamed to say, till the blows were over, and I saw the horrible scenes which ensue on war. I have had quite enough of such sights now, and hope it may not be my lot to be exposed to them again.... We are resting comfortably in our tents, and had a turkey for our Christmas dinner.

****

From Harry Smith's Autobiography

At this moment Gilbert's left was not only checked in its advance, but actually falling back, and I had some difficulty in establishing myself on the front line in consequence of the broken troops falling back upon me. Scarcely was I firmly established, when Major Broadfoot, the Political Agent, rode up and said, "Be prepared, General. Four Battalions of Avitabile's are close upon you in advance; I have it from correct information—a man in my pay has just left them." The smoke and dirt rendered everything at the moment invisible. I saw, however, that to resist this attack, which was evidently made to take advantage of our check, and penetrate our line between Littler's right and Gilbert's left, I must bring up the right of my Brigade. I endeavoured to do so, and with H.M.'s 50th Regiment I partially succeeded, under a storm of musketry and cannon which I have rarely, if ever, seen exceeded. My native troops staggered and some receded, while the gallant old 50th bore the whole brunt, opening a rapid fire. At this moment poor Major Arthur Somerset was struck down, a most accomplished soldier for his experience, and of a promise to emulate his great ancestor the Duke, had Almighty God been pleased to spare him to his country. I never saw a more cool, judicious, and gallant officer than my dear and lamented friend, Arthur Somerset. If the tears of a veteran could decorate the hero's tomb, every vein upon it would be full. Poor youth! *"Sic transit gloria mundi!"*

The enemy was at this moment in his bearing noble and triumphant. So fast were officers and men falling, I saw there was nothing for it but a charge of bayonets to restore the waning fight. I, Colonel Petit, and Colonel Ryan put ourselves at the head of the 50th, and most gallantly did they charge into the enemy's trenches, where such a hand-to-hand conflict ensued as I had never before witnessed. The enemy was repulsed at this point, and his works and cannon carried, and he precipitately retreated.

I pushed forward with the 50th in line until we reached the enemy's camp. All order was broken by the tents, but my orders and example were "Forward! Forward! Forward!"

****

On obeying Harry Smith's orders at the Battle of Ferozeshur by Ensign Innes of the 1st Light Infantry

The soldiers gallantly carried out these orders, but they had not proceeded more than two hundred yards when there was heard beneath their feet a frightful roar; the ground heaved and the men in the vicinity were blown away amongst the tents, the air being filled with fire, and a dense smoke arising, which, as it cleared away, exposed to view a horrible and appalling scene, numbers of our men having fallen frightfully burnt and mutilated, and in some instances their pouches ignited, causing terrible wounds, agony and loss of life.

****

I saw a village occupied by the enemy full in my front, about 400 yards away. By this time I was joined by many stragglers of regiments from my right or Gilbert's Division, but no one from my left or Littler's. I was therefore apprehensive of my left flank, nor was I aware (from the obscurity created by the dust) whether the four Battalions of Avitabile's were repulsed, or indeed where they were. I resolved, therefore, to carry the village, which I soon did in gallant style with H.M.'s 50th and a detachment of the Honourable Company's 1st European Light Infantry under Captain Seaton and Lieutenant —. The colours of H.M.'s 50th were gallantly borne forward by Brevet Captain Lovett and Lieutenant de Montmorency. I was the first officer in the Head-quarters village of the Sikh army, Ferozeshuhur, and I planted one of the colours of H.M.'s 50th on the mud walls. A scene of awful slaughter here ensued, as the enemy would not lay down their arms. The village was full of richly caparisoned and magnificent horses, and there were camels around it innumerable.

After about half an hour the dust cleared away upon my left, and I saw that Avitabile's Battalions had been driven back by my charge, but Littler's Division had made no impression upon the enemy where he attacked. The victory appeared complete on my right; crowds of advancing, straggling officers and soldiers came up, and I resolved again to push forward. The evening was fast closing, but before dark I carried the enemy's camp half a mile beyond the village, and endeavoured to collect and form the stragglers upon H.M.'s 50th—amounting, I conceive, to near 3000 men.

For the first hour, so excited were the men, I could make no formation, which I little regarded at the moment, expecting every instant to hear the victorious army upon my right. Not doing so, on the contrary, hearing the enemy in force close to my front and right (it was very dark), I saw at once I had pushed the victory far beyond, and that my position was critical in the extreme. I therefore made a vigorous and determined exertion to establish a formation, and I got the 24th Regiment Native Infantry—one of my own Division—in line upon my right under Major Bird, and about 150 of the 1st European Light Infantry under Captain Seaton, and proceeded to form the whole in a semicircle in front of the enemy's camp, my flank being well refused towards the village.

Scarcely was this first formation effected, when the enemy made rather a sharp attack upon my right and drove back the formed troops. The darkness prevented the enemy continuing his success, and the noise and clamour of my troops in the endeavour to form indicated that I still held my ground. Thus I was compelled to reoccupy my right and contract the circle of formation. In this arduous duty I (and the Service still more so) was deeply indebted to Major Hull of the 16th Grenadiers, who, after he received a wound of which he died in a few hours, continued to do his duty, and aid me beyond my expression under a murderous fire of musketry, grape, round shot, and *grisaille*.

I at length got all the stragglers, consisting of some of H.M.'s 9th Regiment under Major Barwell, the 19th Grenadiers Native Infantry, the 24th Regiment Native Infantry, the 28th Regiment Native Infantry, the 73rd Regiment Native Infantry and many others, upon the 50th, which was well in hand.

The moon arose, and the night was as bright as day. The enemy soon discovered the weakness and isolation of my force, and gradually closed in upon me, keeping up a most destructive fire.

****

Major W. S. R Hodson of the 1st Bengal European Fusiliers on the Battle of Ferozeshah

The 80th Queen's is, as you know, a Staffordshire regiment, having been raised originally by the Marquis of Anglesey, and has still a great number of Staffordshire men in its ranks. It is a splendid corps, well-behaved in cantonments, and first-rate in action. I lay between them and my present regiment (1st E. B. Fusileers) on the night of the 21st of December, at Ferozeshah, when Lord Hardinge called out "80th! That gun must be silenced."

They jumped up, formed into line, and advanced through the black darkness silently and firmly; gradually we lost the sound of their tread, and anxiously listened for the slightest intimation of their progress, all was still for five minutes, while they gradually gained the front of the battery whose fire had caused us so much loss. Suddenly we heard a dropping fire, a blaze of the Sikh cannon followed, then a thrilling cheer from the 80th, accompanied by a rattling and murderous volley as they sprang upon the battery and spiked the monster gun.

In a few more minutes they moved back quietly, and lay down as before in the cold sand: but they had left forty-five of their number and two captains to mark the scene of their exploit by their graves.

****

THE NIGHT OF THE BATTLE OF FEROZESHAH AND THE PLIGHT OF THE WOUNDED RELATED BY LIEUTENANT JOHN CUMMING OF THE 80TH FOOT

A burning camp on one side of the village, mines and ammunition wagons exploding in every direction, the loud orders given to extinguish the fires as the sepoys lighted them, the volleys given should the Sikhs venture too near, the booming of the monster guns, the incessant firing of the smaller ones, the continued whistling noise of the shell, grape and round shot, the bugles sounding, the drums beating, and the yelling of the enemy, together with intense thirst, fatigue and cold, and not knowing whether the rest of the army were the conquerors or conquered—all contributed to make this night awful in the extreme.

Many a gallant fellow was lying in the square silent, though severely wounded, some of them bleeding to death without a murmur. In the 80th square a grapeshot struck a man in the shoulder, producing a rather severe flesh wound. The foolish fellow wanted to get out of the square: where he intended going I know not, but if he had got his wish he would probably have been cut to pieces. He would not be quiet, but kept telling everyone that he was wounded, as if his wound was of more consequence than that of anyone else. Being refused by a sergeant of his

Company, he went to the Colour-Sergeant saying, "Sergeant, I am badly wounded, let me get out of the square to go to the surgeon."

The Colour-Sergeant replied, "Lie down where you are man, look at me," lifting up a leg without a foot. But he was determined to gain his point, and came to Lieutenant Bythesea, who commanded his company, and was lying next me.

"Oh Sir, I wish you would give orders to let me out of the square: I am wounded."

"So am I," coolly answered Mr Bythesea, putting round his right arm, and lifting up his left hand which hung shattered from the wrist.

Though he was not near me I did not know till then that he had been hurt. But the man persevered and came now to Colonel Bunbury, who commanded the regiment, and was still on horseback. He was about two yards from where I lay.

"Sir," cried the man, "I am wounded, please give orders for me to go and have it dressed."

"So you're wounded, my good man," said the Colonel.

"Yes Sir."

"So am I."

I then perceived that the colonel was wounded just below the knee, and the blood had filled his boot, and was trickling from the heel to the ground. The assistant-sergeant-major had been watching this man, and, becoming angry at the annoyance he was causing, determined to stop it.

He ran up and seized him, saying "Damn—," but before any more was out of his mouth a cannon ball carried away his head, and a part of the unfortunate private's, killing both at once.

Night camp at the battle of Ferozeshah

****

From Harry Smith's Autobiography

My A.A.G. and Q.M.G. were both wounded, their horses killed—every officer and soldier dead-tired, so that many were killed fast asleep, both officers and men. I was fully aware of the importance of my post, in the very centre of and beyond the enemy's entrenched position, and although I could hear nothing of our army or see any bivouac fires, I resolved to maintain myself to the last. The loss, however, became every moment more heavy, and officers and soldiers were restless and sensible of their critically advanced position. The enemy got a gun to bear directly on my rear; my course was decided for me, and I at once saw indications of the impossibility of maintaining myself any longer.

It was now three o'clock in the morning. To withdraw without being compromised was a most perilous operation, for I was surrounded, while the enemy were shouting and cheering, beating up troops, and calling out to us in French and English, as well as Hindoostani, that we were in their power. I therefore feigned to attack, opened a fire and under the smoke quietly drew off, H.M.'s 50th leading. For the last arrangement, this was my reason—if I were opposed, the 50th would charge through such opposition; if pressed on my rear and the native troops rushed past me, I then had a rear-guard of H.M.'s troops which I could depend on. The enemy never discovered my retrograde movement until I was out of his power.

I then marched straight, leaving Ferozeshuhur to my left and continuing my route (guided by the moon and the dead soldiers on the line by which I advanced). I soon fell in with a vedette, and, concluding all was right and seeing a bivouac fire, regarded it as the picquet of cavalry from which he was posted. Upon reaching the fire, I found it belonged to the wounded men of H.M.'s 62nd Regiment and others, under some surgeons, who knew nothing whatever of our army. It was presumptuously urged upon me by several officers, who ought to have thought before they spoke, to move on Ferozepore. My answer was decided enough. "The Commander-in-Chief with his army is not far from us, meditating an attack as soon as it is daylight, and find him I will if in h—ll, where I will join him, rather than make one retrograde step till I have ascertained some fact." At the moment a large flame mounted up, as if soldiers were lighting a large fire. I exclaimed, "There's my point, friend or foe."

In about three-quarters of a mile I reached the fire, the village of Misreewalla, where I found a Brigade of Cavalry, some Irregular Horse, some Horse Artillery, and two or three thousand stragglers of every Regiment in the army.

****

Lieutenant Robertson of the 31st Foot on the confusion of the British withdrawal after the Battle of Ferozeshah

The Sikhs had retired and we had possession of this part of their camp; but instead of holding on to what we had got with so much loss, we were ordered to retire for the night. We then went back in a sort of mob, men of all regiments being mixed together, and every officer shouting for his company or regiment.

One man would say, "Where is the 80th?"

"Here it is," would say another.

"No, this is the 31st," would say a third, and so on.

The colours of two or three regiments were all together, and everyone would have it that he was right. I ran up against Law, who was crying out, "Where is Paul and the colours?" and at last seeing him he held on and railed out, "Here is the 31st; this way 31st, etc," until we got into some sort of order. But there was no firing in front of us then and we thought the battle was over.

We formed at quarter-distance column, and lay down on the cold sand. It was then that we began to feel the most frightful thirst, and not a drop of anything was to be had. I had a little drop of gin in a flask, and took a pull at it, giving the rest to the men with me. But this only made us the worse, and the cold was so intense that we were quite frozen.

****

FROM HARRY SMITH'S AUTOBIOGRAPHY

I halted my people and got hold of some spirits, which I issued to my gallant 50th and all the Europeans. Soon after I reached Misreewalla I met Captain Lumley, A.A.G. of the Army and at the head of the Department (General Lumley being sick, and Major Grant desperately wounded at Moodkee). I was delighted to see him, concluding he came direct from the Commander-in-Chief.

He said, "Sir Harry Smith, you are the very man I am looking for. As senior officer of the Adjutant-General's department, I order you to collect every soldier and march to Ferozepore."

I said, "Do you come direct from the Commander-in-Chief, *with such an order?* If you do, I can find him, for, by G—, I'll take no such order from any man on earth but from his own mouth. Where is he?"

"I don't know, but these in my official capacity are the orders."

"D— the orders, if not the Commander-in-Chief's. I'll give my own orders, and take none of that retrograde sort from any Staff officer on earth. But why to Ferozopore? What's the matter?"

"Oh, the army has been beaten, but we can buy the Sikh soldiers."

"What!" says I, "have we taken no guns?"

"Oh yes," he says, "fifty or sixty."

"Thank you," I said; "I see my way, and want no orders."

Turning round to my A.G., Captain Lugard, I said, "Now get hold of every officer and make him fall in his men."

At this moment Captain Christie, in command of an irregular Corps of Horse, a most excellent officer, came up and said he knew the direction the Commander-in-Chief was in and could point it out. I was delighted, and I marched off every man able to move to join Sir Hugh Gough, sending forward my wounded A.G. to report my whereabouts and what troops I had with me.

The Commander-in-Chief was as delighted to hear of me and my troops as I was to find His Excellency. His orders were to move up in support of the attack which I well and truly anticipated he meditated, when to my astonishment I saw the village of Ferozeshuhur full in my front two miles distant, the very post I had carried and occupied the night before, and from which, after having held it until three o'clock that morning, I was compelled to withdraw, or I should have remained there nearly by myself.

The attack was made on the part of the enemy's camp he still held, namely, his right, which had repulsed Littler's attack on the afternoon of the 21st. It was now carried without a check. The 1st Brigade of my Division, especially H.M.'s 31st Regiment, greatly distinguished itself and suffered severely.

****

The day after the Battle of Ferozeshur related by Lieutenant John Cumming of the 80th Foot

I awoke as the reveille was sounding on the morning of the 23rd to find myself stiff with cold, my clothes covered with hoarfrost and my limbs so benumbed that I could not rise. After my servant had chafed and squeezed them I got on my legs. A walk was necessary to bring me round and I staggered through the entrenched camp—a horrible sight: death was there in its most hideous forms, and men dying in all the most excruciating agonies. Walking about was still dangerous, for the Sikhs' mines were every now and then exploding as fire happened to reach them.

I wandered along in a confused way in search of something. I hardly knew what it was that I wanted. At length behind a curtain in a Sikh tent, I saw a large earthen vessel full of pure cold water. This is what I had been looking for! I flew upon it, and plunged my head and arms into it, clothes and all. I drank till I could drink no more, then stood up and drank again and again.

****

From Harry Smith's Autobiography

Scarcely was the victory of the 21st and 22nd December over, when a fresh body of the enemy (which had been watching Ferozepore or threatening an attack if the garrison was withdrawn, and had been deluded through Littler's very judiciously leaving his camp standing) came vaunting upon the left of our line and opened a fierce cannonade upon us, literally within what had been their own camp and entrenchments.

The ammunition for our guns was fully expended, and our troops were literally exhausted, and we could not attack what would have been an easy prey under other circumstances. The whole of the enemy withdrew and recrossed the Sutlej unmolested, for our troops were in no condition to pursue. Our numerous wounded required to be collected, our stores to be brought up, our troops to be refreshed.

From the march of the troops from Umbala and Loodiana upon Busseean, our men had fought three actions, the battles of Moodkee, Ferozeshuhur, and that of the 22nd December, gained three victories, and endured great fatigue of marching and privations, especially of what is so important to the native troops, water. In a day or two the whole were fresh, and we moved forward on the line the enemy had withdrawn by.

The 1st Division was on the right of the army, and subsequently Brigadier Cureton's Brigade of Cavalry (two troops of Horse Artillery, H.M.'s 16th Lancers, 3rd Light Cavalry, and a corps of Irregular Horse under a Captain Hill) were posted again to my right and under my command. My outposts were opposite the enemy. At Sobraon, which afterwards became so renowned, the enemy threw over a bridge and had a ford near it; they ably constructed *têtes du pont*, and showed an intention to cross. To do so was an act of madness which could not be contemplated by any reasoning faculties, although ultimately demonstrated.

It appeared to me that our army was not posted where it ought to be, and I strongly recommended to the Commander-in-Chief to move up the left bank of the Sutlej, so that his centre should be opposite Sobraon, and his left be kept in direct communication with Ferozepore by an intermediate corps under the command of Sir John Grey, which could also watch the reputed fords and ferries on that part of the river on his front,—the right of the army, namely, my command, Cureton's Cavalry and my own Division, to be posted opposite the ford and ferry of Hurreekee. The Commander-in-Chief called for the distribution of the army as I proposed, which I gave in, accompanied by an explanatory letter to His Excellency. In forty-eight hours it was adopted, and the army moved into the celebrated position opposite Sobraon.

Here the enemy constructed a bridge of boats and pushed over his whole army, most strongly fortifying and entrenching himself on the left side of the river, a movement unparalleled in the history of war from time immemorial. It may be asked, Why was he permitted? Answer, Because we could not help ourselves. The right or enemy's bank was high and favourable for him in every way, and the bridge was judiciously thrown over at a bend of the river; hence the natural formation presented a formidable *tête du pont*, which the enemy entrenched and filled with cannon of the heaviest calibre. We could not contend with him, our heavy guns not having arrived, and the left bank of the river being nearly perfectly flat. Thus he could cross, and did, unmolested, and duly pushed his outposts forward and ours back, until it was deemed necessary to counter-fortify our camp in his front, which was done by bringing some of the heavy guns from Ferozepore. My Division and command being well to the right, I had a line of outposts from the confluence of the Beas and the Sutlej to within a mile of the enemy's entrenchments at Sobraon.

****

FROM A LETTER BY HARRY SMITH
TO HIS SISTER ALICE

Left bank of the Sutlej, 28th December, 1845
Your old brother Harry has only a few minutes to say to you and his dear friend Sir James Kempt he has at length in India had an opportunity of distinguishing himself as much as you both could wish, in the three most sanguinary conflicts with the Sikhs, and he with his own hand, the first man in, planted the

colour of H.M.'s 50th Regiment on the walls of the headquarter village from which the great battle was named, Ferozeshuhur.

A bloody fight it has been, as you will see by the papers. I was with the old 50th hand to hand in their trenches when four battalions of Avitabile's (so called from having been drilled by that officer) bore down in furious onslaught upon my Division which I now command–two Brigades, H.M.'s 31st and two Native Regiments in one, the 50th and two Native Regiments in the other.

In the affair of the 18th my Division took twelve guns and a howitzer; in the great battle, three fine standards; and on the 22nd my Division made a furious charge and completed the victory. I was placed on the night of the 21st in a most critical and perilous position in the very middle of the whole Sikh (though beaten) army, completely surrounded by thousands, and at three o'clock succeeded in drawing off my troops, and received the thanks of Sir H. H.: "Smith, it was your boldness and audacity that *saved* to us the victory."

Poor old General Sale asked leave on the 18th to serve with me. I gave him a Battalion, at the head of which he received his mortal wound. Our loss has been as great in proportion as in our most bloody fights in the Peninsula. All my Staff were wounded, A.A.G. and A.Q.M.G. in two places. My A.D.C., Eliza Holdich's son, wounded in the hand, one horse killed, one wounded. Myself and my horses escaped, with the blessing of Almighty Providence, without a scratch. I was in the saddle from half-past two on the morning of the 21st to four o'clock in the afternoon of the 23rd. My dear, dear gallant young friend Somerset received his mortal wound close to me, and fell in my A.D.C.'s arms. Tell Sir James I will send him next mail copy of my report; this, I cannot. I have no clerks as when A.G. Dear Juana is at Meerut, thank God, well out of the way. Your old humbug of a brother's name *up* in the army, I do assure you, especially with Sir Henry Hardinge and Sir Hugh Gough; Sir H. H. treats and takes and asks my opinion for as much as it is worth, as my dear, dear friend Sir James would.

Heaven bless you, I know this will gratify you and Sir James. So I send this on a thick scrawl of paper. I have not time to read it over.

CHAPTER 6

The Battle of Badowal

FROM HARRY SMITH'S AUTOBIOGRAPHY

On the 16th January the Commander-in-Chief sent for me, and told me the Governor-General was desirous that the small fortress of Futteyghur and the larger one of Dhurmcote, both slightly garrisoned by the enemy, should be reduced, as under their cover he was drawing supplies from the left bank and crossing them over.

His Excellency said, "A Brigade will be sufficient to send, the 3rd Light Cavalry and some Irregular Horse; but who will you send?"

I replied I had rather go myself. Sir Hugh Gough was much pleased with my offering to do so, for I subsequently ascertained it was the Governor-General's desire I should be ordered. The Commander-in-Chief said, "When will you march? there is no hurry."

I said, "Soon after this time to-morrow I shall be writing my report that I have reduced them both."

He laughed and said, "Why, the distance to Dhurmcote is twenty-six miles from your right."

I replied, "I know that; still, what I say shall be, provided that the officer and the Engineers supply me in time with the powder I want to blow in the gates in the case of necessity." I said to myself, "However, powder or no powder, I march."

When I reached camp, I found that, without my knowledge, the Commissariat had sent almost all the tent elephants and other transport into Ferozepore for provisions; some, however, arrived in the night. These provisions I laid hold of, and I collected every animal in camp for the use of the troops ordered to move, and I marched two hours before daylight.

On my approach Futteyghur was abandoned, and I pushed on to Dhurmcote, which I reached by two o'clock in the afternoon, and found it occupied, but without any gun deserving the name of cannon. I invested it immediately with the 3rd Light Cavalry and Irregulars (the infantry not being yet up), and summoned the garrison to surrender. It received my flag of truce, and the leader or *killadar* came out and made a variety of stipulations, which I cut short by saying, "You may march out with your arms, ground them on the glacis, and I will endeavour to secure all hands six weeks' pay. Go back to the fort. I give you 20 minutes to consider, after which I shall make no terms, but open my cannon upon you."

I waited 25 minutes, and no communication being made, although I rode close to the works myself and beckoned to them, I ordered our 9-pounders and a howitzer to open a few shots. The Sikh flag was then hauled down, and a white one hoisted. I allowed the garrison to march out and lay down their arms as prisoners of war, and as the Infantry arrived, I immediately occupied the fortress and commenced improving its defences. I was thus able to report, as I had promised, to my Commander-in-Chief.

I had orders to reconnoitre the country around to ascertain its resources and the feeling of amity or hostility of the neighbourhood. Near me the villages were Mussulman and well disposed. Dhurmcote itself belonged to a Sirdar in the enemy's camp, but the people, when the hand of power was manifested, were civil and brought me all the supplies I required.

Having made so long a march on the 17th and being desirous to put the fortress in a state of defence, I had resolved to halt on the 18th, when I received a communication to say that on the 19th I should receive a reinforcement of two troops of Horse Artillery (*viz.* 12 guns), H.M.'s 16th Lancers, and the remainder of the corps of Irregular Horse under Brigadier Cureton. Upon these reaching me, I should have a Brigade of Cavalry, one of Infantry, and 18 guns. With this force I was to move on to Jugraon, thence open a communication with Busseean, the line nine miles to the interior of Jugraon, on which our enormous battering train, stores, treasure, and ammunition, covering an extent of ten miles of road, was marching. I was informed that I might get hold of H.M.'s 53rd Regiment at Busseean, and if so, they were to obey my orders.

Under any circumstances, I was to open a communication with Loodiana (distant from Jugraon, by the direct roads *viâ* the little fortress of Budowal, twenty-five or twenty-six miles), it being threatened by Runjoor Singh's army of 50 guns and 30,000 men, which had crossed at Philour by boats and was in position at Baranhara, seven miles from Loodiana. The force at Loodiana, under Lieutenant-Colonel Godby, 30th Regiment N.I., consisted of one Regiment, the 5th Native Cavalry, the 30th and 36th Sermoor and Nusseeree Battalions, and four guns Horse Artillery.

On the 19th I marched the Infantry to Koharee, halfway to Jugraon, which divided the distance, and I left orders at Dhurmcote for Colonel Cureton to move on the 20th to Jugraon, where he was to join me, which was effected accordingly.

On reaching Jugraon, I received a report from Lieutenant-Colonel Phillips, commanding H.M.'s 53rd Regiment, to whom I had sent orders to Busseean to move on without delay to Jugraon. He begged a day's halt, representing that his transport was done. I had opened a communication with Colonel Godby commanding at Loodiana. I received the most pressing and urgent reasons for my joining him, and I was equally urged by the Governor-General and the Commander-in-Chief to move on to save Loodiana and drive back the invaders under Runjoor Singh and the Rajah of Ladwa. Hence the necessity to concentrate every soldier I could lay my hands on for the purpose. I therefore sent Lieutenant Smith of the Engineers over from Jugraon to Busseean, with a written order for Colonel Phillips to march immediately—provided it were possible. He marched, and the 16th Lancers and guns had reached me.

When I reached Jugraon on the 20th January, all accounts agreed that the enemy was still at Baranhara, thirty miles from me, between Loodiana and Philour, a fortress of his on the right bank of the Sutlej, under cover of which he had crossed and perfected his invasion; but that he had also occupied with a small garrison the fortress of Budowal, which had been abandoned by the troops of a chief in amity with us, and that he had near it some two or three hundred Horse. He was also known to possess a fortress called Gungrana, regarded as very strong, to my right (that is, its parallel) about ten miles from Budowal into our interior, where there was also Cavalry.

I got hold of the 53rd Regiment on the evening of the 20th, the day I arrived at Jugraon. My force therefore stood thus: eighteen guns, one Regiment of English Cavalry (16th Lancers), one Regiment of Native Light Cavalry, one Regiment of Irregular Horse, two Regiments of British Infantry (H.M.'s 31st and 53rd), 250 convalescents, and two very weak Regiments of Native Infantry (the 24th and 47th).

At Jugraon was a very tenable fortress occupied by the troops of a Rajah considered to be friendly, but in time of war and doubtful success friendship is precarious. I therefore occupied the fortress (or rather its citadel) by two Companies of my Native Infantry, and resolved as soon as the moon was up, *viz.* at half-past twelve, to march on Loodiana, leaving Budowal to my right, *i.e.* by the best, shortest, and direct road, and I ordered all baggage which consisted of *wheel-carriage* transport, to remain behind under the protection of the fort of Jugraon.

Meanwhile, every two hours I dispatched instructions of these my intentions to the officer who commanded at Loodiana, whom I ordered to meet me with his force of four Horse Artillery guns, an excellent and strong Regiment of Native Cavalry, and four good and fresh Regiments of Native Infantry. All the while I believed the enemy's force to be at Baranhara, thirty miles from me, but only seven from Loodiana. My order of march was in writing, also my instructions for the baggage and detail of its guards, and I read them on the afternoon of the 20th to all the officers in command. I marched in the most regular order at the hour appointed, with the desire to leave Budowal to my right, and not move by the interior line, *i.e.* between Gungrana and Budowal, two fortresses in the occupation of the enemy, distant only four miles from *both* my flanks, so that my march would be subject to double interruption.

****

SERGEANT PEARMAN OF THE 3RD LIGHT
DRAGOONS ON DETACHMENT ON
THE MARCH TO BADOWAL

Next morning after breakfast we went out to drill, and while at drill an orderly rode in. It sounded 'Dismiss', and then 'Strike Tents', and in half an hour we were again on the march. No one seemed to know where—no road—over sand and through jungle. Anyway, at about 4 o'clock in the afternoon we could see a large camp, and soon found out it was our own army, under the command of Sir Harry Smith.

One of the 16th Lancers came as our guide into the camp. At 5 o'clock we got our tents and put them up. We made some tea, had a wash and went down to the 16th Lancers to see whom I knew; but at 8 o'clock we were ordered to our own tents to hear General Orders read. These were that the whole camp would get the next day's rations, and march at 12 midnight in one column, and move on to the cantonments at Ludhiana. We got on the march at 1 o'clock a.m. It was very dark and cold for India. We marched all the morning, with only one halt of about half an hour.

At about 10 a.m. on January 21st, 1846, I was looking at our left front, when I saw something glisten in the sun's rays. I said: 'Sergeant-Major Baker, there is the enemy.'

He replied: 'You be damned!'

He had been very drunk just before we marched. He had been down to old mates in the 16th Lancers. He had hardly replied when: 'Bang! Bang!', and two balls whizzed over our heads. A third ball went into a regiment of sepoys and knocked over three or four men. The 53rd was taking ground to the left, when a ball passed through them, striking the ground in front of us, close to me, and bounded over our heads.

At this time we were not loaded, but Major Mythyus, in command, gave the order to load, but several of us could not, as our guns were no use. We now got an order to move to the front, and at that moment a ball came and knocked down five. A corporal of the 80th Regiment had his leg knocked off. He said: 'Comrades, take my purse!' I took his gun and tossed my own away.

We stepped over them, and passed on, but had not got far, when another ball struck Harry Greenbank in the head. It sounded like a band-box full of feathers flying all over us. He was my front-rank man, and his brains nearly covered me. I had to scrape it off my face, and out of my eyes, and Taf Roberts, my left-hand man, was nearly as bad.

Our guns now commenced to fire on the enemy. We still continued the march, sometimes towards the enemy, and at other times towards Ludhiana, men falling every few minutes. No man of the 55rd Regiment, or our own detachment, can ever forget that day: forced marching for some days previous, and marching that day from one a.m. until 5 in the evening over thirty miles and under an Indian sun, with Brown Bess, 120 rounds of Ball Cartridge, and coat at our backs.

We had nothing to drink on the road. Some of the men's tongues were protruding from their mouths. At last the men could go no farther, the enemy cavalry following close on our rear to cut up the stragglers. Sergeant-Major Baker became beat, and lay down. I said: 'For God's sake, George, think of your wife and children.' He had two children.

He looked at me, and said: 'I can't.'

A private named Robson, a fine young man, lay down with him.

****

SERGEANT PEARMAN OF THE 3RD LIGHT DRAGOONS
ON THE ARRIVAL OF THE 16TH LANCERS

We moved on a little. When the cavalry was about to charge us, we were ordered to form square, but were unable to do so. We made one corner, but got confused. Roberts said to me: 'Jack, be steady. We will have one each.' And we both up with our guns.

I had not suffered so much from thirst as some men. Roberts made water in his cap and drank it. Just as we became so confused, the 16th Lancers came down at a trot in open column of Troops, and wheeled into line between us and the enemy, and saved us. If they hadn't, none of our detachment would be here to tell the tale. They trotted towards the enemy's cavalry, but they would not stand for the Lancers. They retired.

The 53rd were at this time nearly all fallen down, but began to rally, and so did we, but not until many of our 200 had fallen down and been killed: Ted Mouse, Henry Hazard and many more—I forget their names.

****

FROM HARRY SMITH'S AUTOBIOGRAPHY

The large force nearly equal to mine was to have approached me from Loodiana, within three miles of Budowal on its own side, on a strong hill and position I well knew of, Sonnact. The natives here were most hostile, and it is an axiom, and a very just one, in the conduct of war, 'distant combinations are not to be relied on.' Hence, although I calculated upon this combination, I did not rely upon it, but adopted my own measures for advance with caution and circumspection, relying alone on my own resources.

When I had marched some sixteen or eighteen miles in the most perfect order of advance to within two miles of Budowal, as day dawned, I received a communication from Colonel Godby that the enemy had marched from Baranhara and was encamped around Budowal with his whole force, and from some villagers I ascertained that the enemy had received considerable reinforcements. I found myself thus close upon him, and he in force. I had one of two alternatives, *viz.* to move on, leaving Budowal to my right and most probably the moving Sikh army on my left—in other words, to force my passage; or to leave Budowal to my left and make a *detour* towards Gungrana. To return to Jugraon I never contemplated, which would have exposed Colonel Godby as previously stated.

The stake at issue was too great, hence I changed my order of march and proceeded with every precaution, leaving the fort of Budowal on my *left*, and with my troops in order of battle by wheeling into line to their left if required. Several times during our night march we had observed rockets firing, as if for signals, and at broad daylight we discovered the enemy preparing to interrupt my newly adopted line of march, though his most ample preparation, as I afterwards discovered, had been made for my reception on the more direct road by which I had originally intended to move, and upwards of forty pieces of cannon pointed there, so perfect was his information.

So soon as the enemy had discovered that I had changed my line of march for the relief of Loodiana, he immediately attempted to interrupt my force by moving parallel to my column through a line of villages which afforded him cover and protection, and by providing him with good roads facilitated his march, while I was compelled to move in order of battle over ploughed fields of deep sand. Hence the head of the enemy's column, principally a large body of cavalry, rapidly outflanked me a mile at least, and his rear of guns and infantry equally so.

****

Sergeant Pearman of the 3rd Light Dragoons
on skirmishes on the road to Ludhiana

At last we got in sight of Ludhiana, three or four miles off, when Sir Harry Smith came to us, and looked at us with tears in his eyes. He said: 'Poor boys, lay down now and rest for a time.'

Sir Harry shot the two guides himself. They were

to have taken us wide of the enemy to Ludhiana, but they took us into the range of the enemy's guns.

Where we lay down, there was a large shallow pond, and into this we all went to drink. There were horses, camels, elephants, men, bullocks all at once. The water was nearly like treacle, but down it went. While this was going on many of the 16th Lancers were fetching in men of the 53rd, and our detachment, on their horses in front of them. By this means they saved many men that, had they not done so, must have been killed. The enemy took all our baggage, and the stores of all the hospitals, killed all our sick and the wounded on the field, and took about twenty prisoners, one of them being Doctor Banyon of the 62nd Foot, who had fallen out from our detachment to see to the wounded men.

One of the men of our Regiment, named Cumber, was taken prisoner. He was stripped naked for their sport, and when naked and being hunted about for sport, he managed to run from them. They fired several times at him, he said. But they missed him. He came to Ludhiana about 10 at night naked. He found his way by following the noise on our march.

That day my meat—I got a piece of meat in the night—was about half cooked, and was the round bone of the shoulder with a piece of meat attached. This I had in my haversack. I sucked this, and that was what stopped my thirst. When I saw the others so bad I passed it along the ranks, each having a suck. It was soon gone. This was all we had that day.

Next morning we called the roll. There were 17 of my regiment's recruits missing, 14 of whom had been killed. Out of our detachment of 200, 47 were missing; 31 were found to be killed, and 16 made prisoners by a man who had charge of the enemy's guns: a deserter from the East India Company's troops in 1836. He had risen to the rank of General of Artillery. This deserter saved the 16 men's lives as prisoners.

Sir Harry Smith came and looked at us on parade on the 22nd, and told us there were no rations to be got. Each man would get two rupees, and do the best he could with them. I and two others went into the town to try and buy something to eat, but we could not get anything.

The natives had got nothing and all the men in camp wanted. I got a ram's head with the wool on. This we took to camp and when we got back we had a pound of elephant's cakes given to each man. I soon eat my lot. One of the men got an earthen pot as large as a pail. This we made use of. We made a fire, put water into the pot, and put it on the fire. We then scorched the wool off the head and washed it, and put it into the earthen pot to cook. It had stewed about two and a half hours, when we heard a great stir in camp and we received orders to strike tents and march. All was now on the stir in quick time. A man named Williams tried to take out the head, when he broke the pot and the broth ran to the ground. He got the thanks of the boys. We then pulled the head to pieces, and the lucky man got a piece. It was so hot, it burnt your mouth, but we got it down and worked at the tents at the same time. We had become used to roughing it. It sounded 'Fall In', so we bundled the tent on to the elephant and ran to the parade ground to fall in, told off, and were on the way again at four miles an hour, quick march.

We now heard the enemy had changed their camp, and we were going to take up their ground, which we did about dusk. The enemy had gone eight or ten miles on to Aliwal. We were now at Badowal, where the battle was fought on the 21st.

Many of the men killed on the 21st were found and buried, and some of the men were found dead in the village of Badowal, where they had been plundered and no doubt killed, as they were naked. We found some of the men's things, and the hospital stores of the 16th Lancers broken up and destroyed. This made the men very angry—and it soon spread at last. Some of the men of the Artillery set fire to some of the houses, which were soon on the ground. In fact we destroyed the place.

On the afternoon of the 23rd a man of ours named Peter Locket—a character—came into camp. He had been left on the ground, dead drunk, when we marched at midnight on January 20th from Jagraon to Badowal, and this was the first we had seen of him. Major Mythyus tried him by a Drumhead Court Martial. He was sentenced to one hundred lashes, which he got that night, and he was put into the 16th Lancer hospital tent.

****

From Harry Smith's Autobiography on the fighting at Badowal

With great celerity he brought to bear on my troops a considerable number of guns of very heavy metal. The cavalry moved parallel with the enemy, and protected from the fire of his guns by a low ridge of sand-hills. My eighteen guns I kept together close in rear of the cavalry, in order to open a heavy fire on the enemy and to check his advance, thereby attracting his attention, so soon as the fortunate moment which I saw approaching arrived.

This fire, which I continued for some ten minutes, had

a most auxiliary effect, creating slaughter and confusion in the enemy's ranks. The enemy's cannonade upon the column of Infantry had been previously to this furious. I had reinforced the baggage guard, and sent orders that it should close up and keep well on the reverse flank and as much ahead as possible. A few round shot ricocheting among the camels, many of the drivers abandoned their animals, and our own followers and the hostile villages in the neighbourhood plundered a part of the baggage: little of it fell into the hands of the enemy's soldiers.

As the column moved on under this cannonade, which was especially furious upon the rear of the Infantry, the enemy, with a dexterity and quickness not to be exceeded, formed a line of seven battalions directly across my rear, with guns in the intervals of battalions, for the purpose of attacking my column with his line. This was a very able and well-executed move, which rendered my position critical and demanded nerve and decision to evade the coming storm. I would willingly have attacked this line, and I formed up a part of the 31st Regiment as a base, when so deep was the sand and so fatigued were my men, I was compelled to abandon the project. I therefore, under this fierce cannonade, changed front on the centre of the 31st Regiment and of the 53rd by what is a difficult move on parade even—a countermarch on the centre by wings. Then became conspicuous the majesty of discipline and bravery. This move was executed as accurately as at a review.

My Native Regiments were very steady, but I now directed the Infantry to march on Loodiana in echelon of Battalions, ready to receive the word 'Halt, Front' (when they would thus confront the enemy's line if he advanced), and the Cavalry to move in echelon of squadrons, the two arms mutually supporting, the guns in rear of the Cavalry. The whole were moving most correctly and the movement was so steady that the enemy, notwithstanding his overwhelming force, did not attack, but stood amazed, as it were, fearing to quit his stronghold of Budowal, and aware that the junction of my force with that of Loodiana was about to be accomplished.

I was astonished, I admit, at hearing nothing from Colonel Godby. I had reason to hope some of my two-hourly dispatches had reached him, and when at daylight I changed the direction of my march on account of the enemy having anticipated me, I sent Lieutenant Holmes with a party of Irregulars, cautioning him to look as sharp to his right on account of Gungrana as to his left. I soon after sent off Lieutenant Swetenham of the 16th Lancers, and a short time later Lieutenant Band Smith of the Engineers. All these officers reached their destination. From the repeated and urgent requests made by Colonel Godby that I should advance to his relief, from *his then knowledge* that the enemy had anticipated me, I had every reason (supposing he had secured no *positive information* of my march from Jugraon or my orders) to expect some co-operation or demonstration in my support, as I moved towards him. On the contrary, my first messenger found his troops only turning out, he having only just received my instructions, and his force did not move off until the firing had commenced, about half-past seven or eight, at a distance of between eight and nine miles—another illustration of the truth of the axiom, 'distant combinations are not to be relied on.' The natural expectation, too, of Colonel Godby's move towards me cramped my manoeuvres, for had I swerved from the line on which I expected his co-operation, his force would have been compromised and in the power of the enemy's weighty attack. The reinforcement of four guns, a strong and fresh Regiment of Cavalry, and four Regiments of fresh Infantry is a powerful reinforcement to a large army; to me it was nearly one-half of the whole. Decision, coolness, and determination effected the junction and relief of Loodiana, while it cut off the enemy from his line of communication with Philour, under which fortress he had crossed the Sutlej.

A want of water in a position near the enemy compelled me to encamp in front of Loodiana, but I established my outposts close upon him, and frequently made strong patrols up to his position, intending, if he dared attempt to interrupt our line of communication *viâ* Busseean (which I did not, although I so closely watched him, anticipate, so close was I upon him, and the fortress of Jugraon before him), to move on, *coûte que coûte*, and attack under any circumstances. Indeed, my combined force would well have enabled me to do so, had I come up with him when on the march and out of his entrenchments.

Meanwhile the Commander-in-Chief, with great foresight and judgment, ordered the second Brigade of my Division, under Brigadier Wheeler, a Regiment of Native Cavalry, the Body Guard, 400 strong, and four guns Horse Artillery, to move from Hurreekee *viâ* Dhurmcote and Jugraon to join me, while a second Brigade under Brigadier Taylor was ordered in support to Dhurmcote, and the Shekawuttee Brigade was moving on Jugraon. Thus the enemy's position at Budowal was menaced on three points.

He expected considerable reinforcements *viâ* the Tulwun Ghaut, eight miles lower down the Sutlej than Philour. He therefore, again with judgment, abandoned his position of Budowal, in which I was making vigorous preparations to attack him, and fell back upon the reinforcement of 12 guns and 4000 of Regular Infantry of Avitabile's Corps and a large addition of Cavalry. This movement, however, must have been premeditated, for the stores of ammunition and his fortifications around the ford were not the work of a day. I immediately occupied the enemy's position at Budowal, and as rapidly as possible concentrated my force coming from Dhurmcote and Busseean (*viz*.: Wheeler's from the former, and the Shekawuttee from the latter), while I dispensed with the service of Brigadier Taylor's Brigade in reserve at Dhurmcote, feeling myself now sufficiently strong, and being aware of the importance of Infantry to the Commander-in-Chief, who to reinforce me had considerably reduced his own means in the immediate front of the main army of the Sikhs.

This is the *précis* of the campaign leading to the Battle of Aliwal, and from this period taken up in my report of that glorious battle, herewith annexed.

CHAPTER 7

The Battle of Aliwal

FROM SIR HARRY SMITH'S REPORT TO
THE ADJUTANT-GENERAL OF THE ARMY,
ALIWAL, JAN. 30, 1846

My despatches to his Excellency the Commander-in-Chief of the 23rd instant, will have put his Excellency in possession of the position of the force under my command, after having formed a junction with the troops at Loodiana, hemmed in by a formidable body of the Sikh army under Runjoor Singh and the Rajah of Ladwa. The enemy strongly entrenched himself around the little fort of Budhowal by breastworks and 'abattis,' which he precipitately abandoned on the night of the 22nd instant (retiring, as it were, upon the ford of Tulwun), having ordered all the boats which were opposite Philour to that Ghat. This movement he effected during the night, and, by making a considerable detour, placed himself at a distance of ten miles, and consequently out of my reach. I could, therefore, only push forward my cavalry as soon as I had ascertained he had marched during the night, and I occupied immediately his vacated position. It appeared subsequently he had no intention of recrossing the Sutlej, but moved down to the Ghat of Tulwun (being cut off from that of Philour, by the position my force occupied after its relief of Loodiana), for the purpose of protecting the passage of a very considerable reinforcement of twelve guns and 4000 of the regular, or 'Aieen' troops, called Avitabile's battalion, entrenching himself strongly in a semicircle, his flanks resting on a river, his position covered with from forty to fifty guns (generally of large calibre), howitzers, and mortars. The reinforcement crossed during the night of the 27th instant, and encamped to the right of the main army.

Meanwhile, his Excellency the Commander-in-Chief, with that foresight and judgment which mark the able general, had reinforced me by a considerable addition to my cavalry, some guns, and the 2nd brigade of my own Division, under Brigadier Wheeler, C.B. This reinforcement reached me on the 26th, and I had intended the next morning to move upon the enemy in his entrenchments, but the troops required one day's rest after the long marches Brigadier Wheeler had made.

I have now the honour to lay before you the operations of my united forces on the morning of the eventful 28th January, for his Excellency's information. The body of troops under my command having been increased, it became necessary so to organize and brigade them as to render them manageable in action. The cavalry under the command of Brigadier Cureton, and horse artillery under Major Lawrenson, were put into two brigades; the one under Brigadier MacDowell, C.B., and the other under Brigadier Stedman. The 1st Division as it stood, two brigades—Her Majesty's 53rd and 30th Native Infantry, under Brigadier Wilson, of the latter corps;—the 36th Native Infantry, and Nusseree battalion, under Brigadier Godby—and the Shekawattee brigade under Major Forster. The Sirmoor battalion I attached to Brigadier Wheeler's brigade of the 1st division; the 42nd Native Infantry having been left at head-quarters.

At daylight on the 28th, my order of advance was—the Cavalry in front, in contiguous columns of squadrons of regiments, two troops of horse artillery in the interval of brigades; the infantry in contiguous columns of brigades at intervals of deploying distance; artillery in the intervals, followed by two 8-inch howitzers on travelling carriages, brought into the field from the fort of Loodiana by the indefatigable exertions of Lieutenant-Colonel Lane, Horse Artillery; Brigadier Godby's brigade, which I had marched out from Loodiana the previous evening, on the right; the Shekawattee infantry on the left; the 4th Irregular Cavalry considerably to the right, for the purpose of sweeping the banks of the wet nullah on my right, and preventing any of the enemy's horse attempting an inroad towards Loodiana, or any attempt upon the baggage assembled round the fort of Budhowal.

****

ENSIGN TOM PEARCE ON MARCHING TO ALIWAL

. . . . we marched on through fertile country, through forests of magnificent trees with the Jumna murmuring its way through the middle of them and the peafowl and paroquets trying to outdo each other in screaming.

While marching up, we were busy getting perfect with the new percussion drill. The men like them much better than the flintlock ones. They never took a bold aim with them, as they were afraid of a piece of flint flying into their eyes.

****

PRIVATE BALDWIN OF H.M. 9TH REGIMENT OF FOOT
ON THE ARRIVAL OF THE 16TH LANCERS AT ALIWAL

The 16th Lancers are the finest set of men I have ever seen out of London. During the engagement at Aliwal we were still at Bootawallah, watching the Seikh grand army at Sobraon. Here Sir Hugh Gough

The 16th Lancers charging at the battle of Aliwal

was indefatigable in his duty; I have seen him riding about at all times in the night watching the enemy's motions with his night glass.

****

STAFF SERGEANT N. W. BANCROFT OF THE BENGAL HORSE ARTILLERY ON THE CAVALRY AND HORSE ARTILLERY AT ALIWAL

The Cavalry, the 16th Lancers, their parti-coloured pennons fluttering, and their magnificent appearance exciting the admiration of all who saw them, friend or foe; the Irregular Horse, in dark-blue and gold; the 1st Light Cavalry, &c, &c, in the well-known inevitable silver-grey trimmed with scarlet, of the company's service, deployed by squadrons into line, and moved on easily, as the ground was perfectly open, hard and covered with grass. The horse artillery dressed in their usual leather breeches and long boots, and their uniform of blue trimmed with scarlet and gold, took ground, gradually to the right and left as they advanced, thus covering the heads of the infantry columns, which now also deployed into line, steadily, with bayonets fixed and colours flying. The artillery were massed on the flanks and in the centre; there was no dust, for the country round about was green and grassy, and the January sun shone with almost unclouded brilliance; hence, when the army, on an attempt of Runjoon Singh to turn its flank, broke into open column again to take ground to the right, "manœuvres, which," Sir Harry states, "were performed with the precision of the most correct field-day, the battle was most imposing."

****

From Sir Harry Smith's Report to
the Adjutant-General of the Army,
Aliwal, Jan. 30, 1846

In this order the troops moved forward towards the enemy, a distance of six miles, the advance conducted by Captain Waugh, 16th Lancers, the Deputy Assistant Quarter-Master of Cavalry, Major Bradford, of the 1st Cavalry, and Lieutenant Strachey of the Engineers, who had been jointly employed in the conduct of patroles up to the enemy's position, and for the purpose of reporting upon the facility and point of approach. Previously to the march of the troops it had been intimated to me by Major Mackeson, that the information by spies led to the belief the enemy would move somewhere at daylight, either on Jugraon, my position of Budhowal, or Loodiana. On a near approach to his outposts, this rumour was confirmed by a spy, who had just left the camp, saying the Sikh army was actually in march towards Jugraon. My advance was steady; my troops well in hand; and if he had anticipated me on the Jugraon road, I could have fallen upon his centre with advantage.

From the tops of the houses of the village of Poorein, I had a distant view of the enemy. He was in motion and appeared directly opposite my front on a ridge, of which the village of Aliwal may be regarded as the centre. His left appeared still to occupy its ground in the circular entrenchment; his right was brought forward and occupied the ridge. I immediately deployed the cavalry into line, and moved on. As I neared the enemy, the ground became most favourable for the troops to manœuver, being open and hard grass land.

I ordered the cavalry to take ground to the right and left by brigades; thus displaying the heads of the infantry columns; and, as they reached the hard ground, I directed them to deploy into line. Brigadier Godby's brigade was in direct echelon to the rear of the right; the Shekawattee infantry in like manner to the rear of my left; the cavalry in direct echelon on, and well to the rear of, both flanks of the infantry; the artillery massed on the right and centre and left. After deployment, I observed the enemy's left to outflank me, I therefore broke into open column and took ground to my right When I had gained sufficient ground, the troops wheeled into line. There was no dust, the sun shone brightly. These manoeuvres were performed with the celerity and precision of the most correct field day.

****

SERGEANT PEARMAN OF THE 3RD LIGHT DRAGOONS, ON DETACHMENT WITH THE HORSE ARTILLERY, ON THE COMMENCEMENT OF THE BATTLE OF ALIWAL

Those who could ride well were to be taken to Colonel Alexander's Troop of Horse Artillery, to do duty, as the Troop had lost many men and was short of them.

On the morning of January 28th, between 5 & 6 o'clock, Adjutant Smyth, called 'Little Jacky' Smyth, of the 16th Lancers, took us through the camp in the dark. All was confusion, with camels and men and regiments getting together. At last we found Colonel Alexander's Bengal Troop of Horse Artillery, when Adjutant Smyth hollered out to Alexander—he stammered in his speech—'Here,' he said,'take these young devils, for I am Adjutant, Quartermaster-General and everything else this morning. Goodbye, Colonel'; and away he went.

Colonel Alexander said, 'Can these boys ride?'

Sergeant Darling replied:'All of them.'

The Colonel then said to Sergeant Douglas of the Artillery:'Mount them, and let's get on the road.'

We were soon on the horses' backs and trotted to the front alongside the 16th Lancers, who threw out skirmishers to the front.

We marched in three contiguous columns in battle array. Our gun no. 2 in front, followed by two more, and two behind them, and then the spare horses ridden by the black syces or horse-keepers; About half past eight in the morning we came in sight of the enemy. We came to a halt, and the infantry and foot artillery began to get into a line, spreading out like a lady's fan. It was a beautiful plain for miles. The sun was bright and clear.

There was the enemy in our front, three or four miles long. Our army came into line as steady as a field day. I sat on my horse and looked at the two armies. It was a lovely sight. It sounded 'Advance', and on we moved. I could see the skirmishers of the 16th Lancers were firing their carbines, and at 10 minutes to 10 a.m. the first shot, about a 9-pounder, passed over our heads. It sounded 'Skirmishers In' and back they came at a trot. On we went covered by the 16th Lancers.

At about 700 yards from the enemy, the Colonel shouted: 'Action! Front! Unlimber and prepare for action! Nos. 1 & 2 to the right; 3 & 4 to the front; 5 & 6 to the left.'

We all dismounted and held the horses, when 'bang' went our guns. About the third shot I saw was making holes in the ranks in front of us. We remained more than half an hour in this way when we limbered up, mounted our horses, and with the 16th Lancers and the 3rd Native Cavalry, took ground to the left, more than a mile past the 53rd Foot, which was in the left-hand infantry brigade, near to a nullah or deep water-course.

An officer of the 16th Queen's Lancers

At this time the firing was terrific, and looking back, the plain was covered with wounded and dead men, and horses and pieces of broken guns. Just at the time we were going to dismount, a shot struck my horse, and down he went with me. I was not hurt.

We were in a cross fire from the enemy's guns and we had seven horses down at once in my gun (no. 5), out of the eight horses. We had lost several men and they were getting short, and so were the horses. A ball struck Private Steele of ours in the head, and down he went. Our man who rode next to the gun had both legs cut off with a ball through the horse.

We limbered up again and I and Jack Reeves rode on ammunition boxes, when a shot came and struck the wheel close to me, smashed it, and the spoke struck Reeves in the thigh, but did not hurt him much. It all missed me. We had to put on a spare wheel and on we went again with fresh horses from the rear, brought up by the black syces or horse-keepers. We now galloped close to the enemy, about three hundred yards, and 'Bang! Bang!' went our guns to a good tune and they did something to think about.

****

FROM SIR HARRY SMITH'S REPORT TO
THE ADJUTANT-GENERAL OF THE ARMY,
ALIWAL, JAN. 30, 1846

The glistening of the bayonets and swords of this order of battle was most imposing; and the line advanced. Scarcely had it moved 150 yards, when, at ten o'clock, the enemy opened a fierce cannonade from his whole line. At first his balls fell short, but quickly reached us. Thus upon him, and capable of better ascertaining his position, I was compelled to halt the line, though under fire, for a few moments, until I ascertained that, by bringing up my right and carrying the

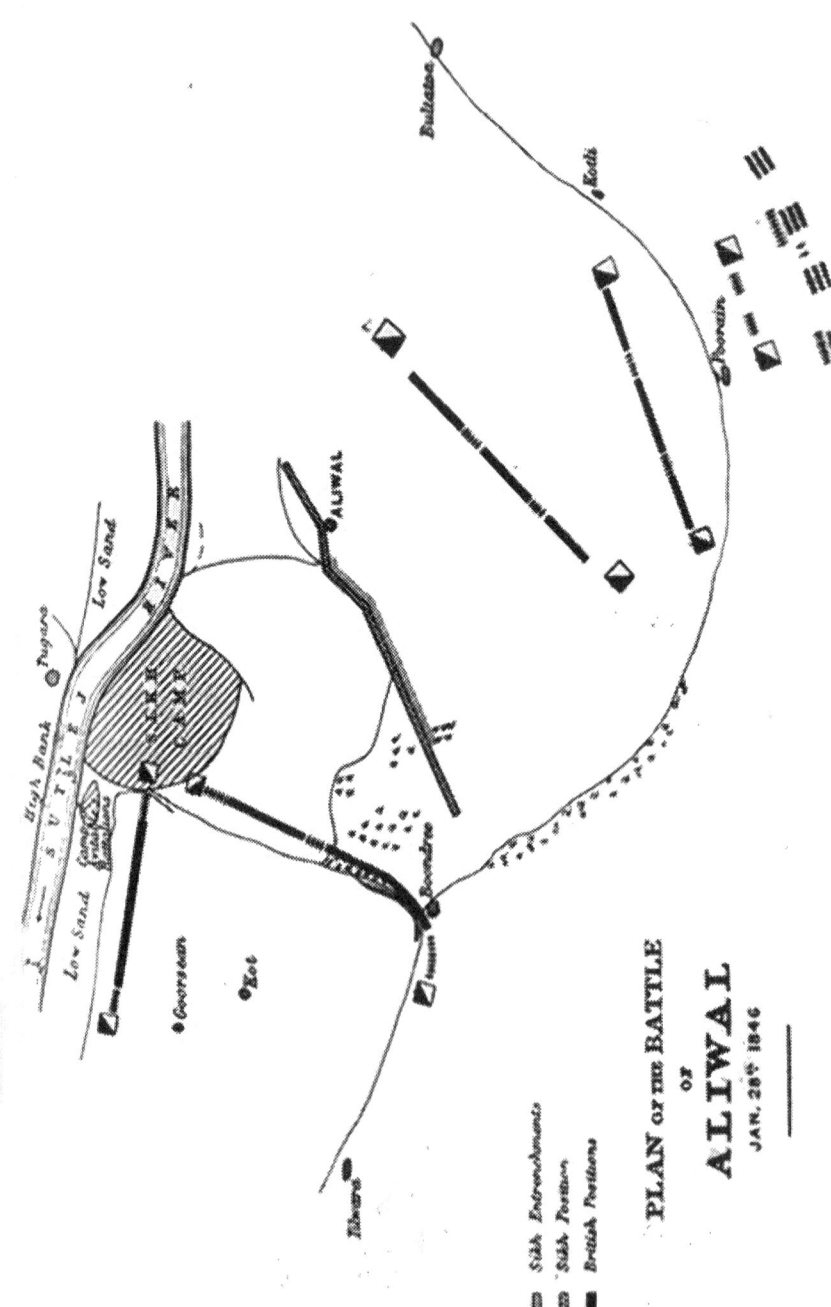

Plan of the Battle of Aliwal—January 28th, 1846

village of Aliwal, I could with great effect precipitate myself upon his left and centre.

I therefore quickly brought up Brigadier Godby's brigade; and, with it, and the 1st brigade under Brigadier Hicks, made a rapid and noble charge, carried the village, and two guns of large calibre. The line I ordered to advance—Her Majesty's 31st Foot and the native regiments contending for the front; and the battle became general. The enemy had a numerous body of cavalry on the heights to his left, and I ordered Brigadier Cureton to bring up the right brigade of cavalry, who, in the most gallant manner, dashed in among them and drove them back upon their infantry.

Meanwhile a second gallant charge to my right was made by the light cavalry and the body-guard. The Shekawattee brigade was moved well to the right, in support of Brigadier Cureton, when I observed the enemy's encampment and saw it was full of infantry: I immediately brought upon it Brigadier Godby's brigade, by changing front, and taking the enemy's infantry en reverse. They drove them before them, and took some guns without a check.

While these operations were going on upon the right, and the enemy's left flank was thus driven back, I occasionally observed the brigade under Brigadier Wheeler, an officer in whom I have the greatest confidence, charging and carrying guns and everything before it, again connecting his line, and moving on, in a manner which ably displayed the coolness of the Brigadier and the gallantry of his irresistible brigade—Her Majesty's 50th Foot, the 48th Native Infantry, and the Sirmoor battalion—although the loss was, I regret to say, severe in the 50th.

Upon the left, Brigadier Wilson, with Her Majesty's 53rd and the 30th Native Infantry equalled in celerity and regularity their comrades on the right; and this brigade was opposed to the 'Aieen' troops, called Avitabile's, when the fight was fiercely raging.

The enemy, well driven back on his left and centre, endeavoured to hold his right to cover the passage of the river, and he strongly occupied the village of Bhoondree. I directed a squadron of the 16th Lancers, under Major Smyth and Captain Pearson, to charge a body to the right of a village, which they did in the most gallant and determined style, bearing everything before them, as a squadron under Captain Bere had previously done, going right through a square in the most intrepid manner with the deadly lance. This charge was accompanied by the 3rd Light Cavalry under Major Angelo, and as gallantly sustained.

****

Captain Knight of the 16th Lancers on their famous charge at Aliwal

Away we went, and as we cleared the trenches with a bound, the enemy were lanced by our men at their guns. We suddenly found ourselves in the midst of a fearfully large square of the enemy's infantry, firing at us right and left and completely surrounding us. The moment that I felt my horse leap the ditch in which their battery was placed and found myself charging into the square . . . . a proud sensation of delight came over me . . . . everything seemed charged into a thrill of ecstasy; and how we all escaped the deadly shower of musketry that was poured into us on all sides is wonderful.

One fellow discharged his gun right across my face and for the moment I was quite blinded by the gunpowder, and my face so blackened no one knew me, and the bullet from another matchlock grazed my fingers and killed the man on my left. Meick, who commanded our squadron, was attacked by a Seikh who put his musket to his side, and would have discharged it through him, but luckily Meick gave it a push and the ball went through the neck of his horse. Everyone who charged with the 16th must have had narrow escapes, for the bullets hissed over our heads like hail. Here poor Swetenham was killed almost close to me, and our brave leader Major Smyth terribly wounded by a musket shot in the thigh. Pottle was also shot in the cheek and only just escaped losing an eye.... Our brave fellows fell very thickly here, and every man whose horse was killed was to a certainty slain also, for the moment those savages saw any one on the ground they rushed at him and never ceased hacking at them, till they had literally severed them to pieces with their tulwars, which were like razors. All of us that escaped owe their lives, under God, to our horses, for no one escaped who once came to the ground. After having charged through this mass of infantry we rallied and pursued the stragglers to the very banks of the river. Poor Williams fell, mortally wounded. Orme was also bayoneted in the stomach and, we fear, may not survive. Captain Tyler is also severely wounded and is likely to lose a leg, and Captain Bere and Lieutenant Yule are both much cut up and bruised.

****

SERGEANT PEARMAN OF THE 3RD LIGHT DRAGOONS
ON THE CHARGE OF THE 16TH LANCERS AT ALIWAL

At this time I looked to our left and saw the 16th Lancers coming on at a trot, then a gallop. I took off my cap and hollered out: 'The first charge of British Lancers!'. The enemy formed square, but the 16th Lancers went right on it and broke it. Such cutting and stabbing I never saw before or since.

****

From Sir Harry Smith's Report to the Adjutant-General of the Army, Aliwal, Jan. 30, 1846

The largest gun upon the field, and seven others, were then captured, while the 53rd Regiment carried the village by the bayonet, and the 30th Native Infantry wheeled round to the rear in a most spirited manner. Lieut.-Col. Alexander's and Capt. Turton's troops of horse artillery, under Major Lawrenson, dashed among the flying infantry, committing great havoc, until about 800 or 1000 men rallied under the high bank of a nullah, and opened a heavy but ineffectual fire from below the bank. I immediately directed the 30th Native Infantry to charge them, which they were able to do upon their left flank, while in a line in rear of the village. This native corps nobly obeyed my orders and rushed among the Avitabile troops, driving them from under the bank and exposing them once more to a deadly fire of twelve guns within 300 yards.

****

The Battle of Aliwal as related by Ensign Tom Pearce

We reached the summit of a high hill and came to an extensive level plain . . . . and about eighteen hundred yards ahead was the Sikh army in battle array, drawn up in line, guns in front, drums beating . . . . Our troops had only just time to deploy in line before they boomed forth their murderous fire.

The first man that was killed stood only a few yards from me. A 9-pound shot took his head from his body. I felt rather sick at seeing the men fall by threes and fours around me. 'Forward and lie down!' came the word of command.

Forward we went by about forty yards at a time, then lay down on the ground, allowing the balls to pass

A charge of the 3rd Light Dragoons

over us .... Then when his fire became slack, forward again for another fifty yards and so on .... our artillery on the right blazing away as hard as they could .... On and on we went in this manner for about an hour. By this time we were eight hundred yards from their battery and could see, through the clouds of smoke, their infantry and horse drawn up in rear of their guns. They now began to flay us with grape and chain shot, which at first thinned our ranks a little.

The enemy hesitated under our severe cannonading, which by this time had greatly silenced them. All of a sudden the whole of our line from right to left gave a wild hurrah and rushed forward, the enemy flying like chaff before the wind, leaving their guns upon the field which were at once spiked by us.

****

SERGEANT PEARMAN OF THE 3RD LIGHT DRAGOONS ON THE END OF THE BATTLE OF ALIWAL

I ran and picked up a man named Wise, shot in the leg, and put him on our gun carriage. I then ran and picked up Sergeant Stearger, shot in the neck, and put him on the gun carriage with Wise. These two men belonged to the 16th Lancers. Then we opened fire again at the broken ranks with grape and canister shot which made great havoc.

Their army now seemed to be in full retreat towards the river, where there was a shallow ford which took them to the fortress of Valore. But before they could get over the ford we had taken all their guns—67. One that was nearly over the river, in the ford, our No. 2 gun fired a shot at and knocked off its limber into the water. That made 68 guns. There were 5 guns taken by us, and the one in the water made 6 for the Troop.

****

From Sir Harry Smith's Report to the Adjutant-General of the Army, Aliwal, Jan. 30, 1846

The destruction was very great, as may be supposed, from guns served as these were. Her Majesty's 53rd Regiment moved forward in support of the 30th Native Infantry, by the right of the village. The battle was won; our troops advancing with the most perfect order to the common focus—the passage of the river. The enemy, completely hemmed in, were flying from our fire, and precipitating themselves in disordered masses into the ford and boats, in the utmost confusion and consternation; our 8-inch howitzers soon began to play upon their boats, when the debris of the Sikh army appeared upon the opposite and high bank of the river, flying in every direction, although a sort of line was attempted to countenance their retreat, until all our guns commenced a furious cannonade, when they quickly receded.

Nine guns were on the river by the ford. It appears as if they had been unlimbered to cover the ford. These being loaded, were fired once upon our advance; two others were sticking in the river, one of them we got out; two were seen to sink in the quicksands; two were dragged to the opposite bank and abandoned. These, and the one in the middle of the river, were gallantly spiked by Lieutenant Holmes, of the 11th Irregular Cavalry, and Gunner Scott, of the 1st troop 2nd brigade Horse Artillery, who rode into the stream, and crossed for the purpose, covered by our guns and light infantry.

Thus ended the battle of Aliwal, one of the most glorious victories ever achieved in India, by the united efforts of Her Majesty's and the Honourable Company's troops. Every gun the enemy had fell into our hands, as I infer from his never opening one upon us from the opposite bank of the river, which is high and favourable for the purpose—fifty-two guns are now in the Ordnance Park; two sank in the bed of the Sutlej; and two were spiked on the opposite bank; making a total of fifty-six pieces of cannon captured or destroyed. Many jingalls which were attached to Avitabile's corps and which aided in the defence of the village of Bhoondree, have also been taken.

The whole army of the enemy has been driven headlong over the difficult ford of a broad river; his camp, baggage, stores of ammunition and of grain—his all, in fact, wrested from him, by the repeated charges of cavalry and infantry, aided by the guns of Alexander, Turton, Lane, Mill, Boileau, and of the Shekawattee brigade, and by the 8-inch howitzers—our guns literally being constantly ahead of everything.

The determined bravery of all was as conspicuous as noble. I am unwont to praise when praise is not merited; and I here most unavowedly express my firm opinion and conviction, that no troops in any battle on record ever behaved more nobly—British and native, no distinction; cavalry, all vying with H.M.'s 16th Lancers, and striving to head in the repeated charges. Our guns and gunners, officers and men, may be equalled, but cannot be excelled, by any artillery in the world. Throughout the day no hesitation—a bold and intrepid advance—and thus it is that our loss is comparatively small, though I deeply regret to say, severe. The enemy fought with much resolution; they maintained frequent rencontres with our cavalry hand to hand. In one charge, upon infantry, of H.M.'s 16th Lancers, they threw away their muskets and came on with their swords and targets against the lance.

The fort of Goongrana has, subsequently to the battle, been evacuated, and I yesterday evening blew up the fort of Budhowal. I shall now blow up that of Noorpoor. A portion of the peasantry, viz. the Sikhs, appear less friendly to us, while the Mussulmans rejoice in being under our Government.

My loss during the 21st January was, of killed and wounded and sick taken, upwards of 200 men, but many of our wounded and exhausted Infantry were brought off in the Artillery carriages and by the noble exertions of H.M.'s 16th Lancers, who dismounted and put the sick and wounded upon their horses. My orders to the baggage guard (composed of 400 Irregular Horse, to which I afterwards added one squadron of Regular Native Cavalry) were only half obeyed, or our loss of baggage would have been next to nothing; but young soldiers are excited under a heavy cannonade and apprehend more of its deadly effect than I have ever seen the heaviest cannonade (not grape and canister) merit.

****

SERGEANT PEARMAN OF THE 3RD LIGHT DRAGOONS ON THE AFTERMATH OF THE BATTLE OF ALIWAL

We retired back to where they had camped, and there found all the articles that had been stolen from the officers' bungalows at Lhudiana before they set them on fire. I took off my dirty things and put on clean ones from a Camel Trunk belonging to the 56th Foot. I also found a dozen bottles of brandy, but Colonel Alexander made me break them.

We picked up the wounded and then got an old Sikh tent and put it up. We got our food and grog and had a sleep and felt alright. In the evening the black servant brought me the late Sergeant-Major Baker's pony. When me and Harry Proud of the 16th Lancers went into the enemy's old camp to see what we could make, I rode the pony, and Proud walked. We had been at it about half an hour, and had loaded the pony with silk gutteree and other things. I held them down on the pony in front of me.

I saw a Sikh soldier crawling towards Proud, when I called out: 'Look, Harry!', who turned round and gave him a blow on the head. He lay very quiet after that.

We then went down to our old Sikh tent where some of the 16th Lancers were, and gave them some of the things, and some we parted with for grog. I tied the pony up and put the saddle under my head and lay down on one of the silk gutteree, a luxury at those times. I was soon asleep and when I awoke in the morning the pony was gone. Some of the bright boys had been about before me and sold it, and were spending the money. I gave the saddle away.

About midday I was very nearly shot. A private named Goodwin and me took a walk and were looking at the field and the dead. I had just cut off the hair and part of the scalp of a dead Sikh to make a Black Plume, and was looking at a very large dead man, near 7 feet high, and large with it, when someone fired a shot from the town of Aliwal, which struck the ground about a foot from me. So we made off to camp again and got our dinner.

We had a standing camp for three or four days, and then we moved again up the country, marching sometimes right and sometimes left.

****

From Sir Harry Smith's Autobiography

This short but most eventful campaign was one of great difficulty and embarrassment for the General (or myself). The enemy was concentrated, whilst my force was to accumulate contingent on a variety of combinations distant and doubtful.

The political importance of my position was extreme. All

India was at gaze, and ready for anything. Our army—truth must out—most anxious, the enemy daringly and exultingly regarding himself invincible, as the bold and most able and energetic move of Runjoor Singh with his whole force throwing himself between my advance from Jugraon viâ Budowal to Loodiana most fully demonstrated. It is the most scientific move made during the war, whether made by accident or design, and had he known how to profit by the position he had so judiciously occupied, he would have obtained wonderful success. He should have attacked me with the same vigour his French tutors would and would have destroyed me, for his force compared to mine was overwhelming; then turned about upon the troops at Loodiana, beaten them, and sacked and burnt the city—when the gaze I speak of in India would have been one general blaze of revolt! Does the world which argues on my affair at Budowal suppose I was asleep, and had not in clear perspective a full view of the effect such success of the enemy would have had upon the general features and character of the war? It must be remembered that our battering train, an immense treasure, our ammunition, etc., etc., were not ten miles from me, occupying a line of road of ten miles in length.

The end was accomplished, viz. the battle of Aliwal and its results. In a few days after the victory I received from my Political Associate, Major Murchison, a very clever fellow, a long report, of which this is an extract:

I cannot help mentioning to you that the result of your decisive victory of the 18th has been the abandonment by the enemy of all his posts south of the Sutlej from Hurreekee upwards to Nunapoor Mackohoorvara, and the submission to our rule of a country yielding an annual revenue of upwards of twenty-five lacs of rupees. The post of the enemy at Sobraon is now the only one held by the Sikhs south of the Sutlej.

The Battle of Aliwal

And again, in a letter from Colonel Godby after he had crossed into the Jullundur with Brigadier Godby:

I have no doubt the battle of Aliwal will be esteemed in England as it deserves; it finished a most painful crisis both in India and in England, and its moral effect in Hindostan and the Punjaub was greater than any other achievement of the war. In the Jullundur the natives speak of it as most unaccountable that the soldiers they thought invincible should be overthrown and driven into the river in two or three hours, and be seen scampering through the country before the people had heard of their defeat. The defeat was so cleanly and unquestionably done, that they ascribed it to supernatural intervention for the many atrocious crimes of the Sikhs, especially upon the oppressed followers of the true Prophet.

All men, especially Generals, reflect in times of peace and quiet upon their exertions, their enterprises, and the measures they adopted. Human life once extinct is in this world gone, and how gratifying it is under Divine Providence to feel that not a soldier under my command was wantonly, unnecessarily, or unscientifically sacrificed to his country! Had I adopted any other course at Budowal on the 21st of January than I pursued, had I not pushed the war entrusted to my conduct with vigour and effected a junction with the troops at Loodiana, they and the city would have fallen, and next our treasure, battering train, ammunition, etc., would have been captured or scattered and lost to the army; had I sustained a serious reverse, all India would have been in a blaze.

I steered the course invariably pursued by my great master the Duke, never needlessly to risk your troops or fight a battle without an object. Hence the decisive victory of Aliwal and its wonderful results and important aid in repelling the Sikh army at Sobraon and seizing the capital of his vaunted glory.

Months have now passed since I conducted these operations, and although reflection as a guide for the future prompts me to find fault with any movement or march, I cannot, but with the blessing of the Almighty, I say, "Results even cannot dictate to me—if you had done this or that, it would have been better."

Having disposed of my captured cannon (I sent forty-seven to the fortress of Loodiana, and took five with me to Headquarters, the most beautiful guns imaginable, which will, I believe, be placed in St. James's Park, London), provided for my sick and wounded, replenished my ammunition and stores, given over to Brigadier Wheeler the troops he was to command on the Upper Sutlej, and furnished him and the Political Agent, Major Murchison, with my views of their operations as a guide.

****

From a letter by Harry Smith to his sister Alice

Camp on the Field of Battle, Aloowal, 1st February, 1846: I have only one moment to say I have gained, in a separate command of 2700 cavalry, 32 guns, and 9000 infantry, one of the most glorious battles ever fought in India, driving the enemy over the Sutledge double my numbers, posted in an intrenched camp with 75 guns, 52 of which are at my tent door, the others lost in the passage of the river, or spiked in its bed. Not a gun did they get over. And oh, the fearful sight the river presents! the bodies having swollen float of men, horses, camels, bullocks, etc. Thousands must have perished, many threw away their arms and fled headlong into the broad river and difficult ford. They had about fifty large boats, which added to the confusion. Some of them were sunk, my thirty-two pieces of cannon pounding them all. Never was victory more complete and never was one fought under more happy circumstances, literally with the pomp of a field-day; and right well did all behave. I brought well into action each arm as auxiliary to the other, but see my dispatch, which will be published as soon as you get this. I have not a moment to write. Send this to dear Sir James Kempt, and tell him my being thus distinguished I owe entirely to his friendship and good opinion of me. Send this to him, for I have not a moment to write.

The Battle of Aliwal

Nominal Roll of Officers Killed and Wounded. 28th January.

First Brigade of Cavalry.

H. M.'s 16th Lancers—Lieutenant H. Swetenham, killed; Cornet G. B. Williams, killed; Major J. R. Smyth, severely wounded; Captain E. B. Bere, wounded; Captain L. Fyler, severely wounded; Lieutenant W. K. Orme, severely wounded; Lieutenant T. Pattle, wounded; Lieutenant W. Morris, wounded.

4th Irregular Cavalry—Lieutenant and Adjutant Smalpage, killed.

Second Brigade of Cavalry.

1st Regiment Light Cavalry—Cornet W. S. Beatson, slightly wounded; Cornet T. G. Farquhar, mortally wounded.

First Brigade of Infantry.

H. M.'s 31st Regiment—Lieutenant Atty, slightly wounded.
24th Regiment N. Infantry—Lieutenant Scott, wounded.

Second Brigade Infantry.

Brigade Major Captain P. O'Hanlon, badly wounded.

H. M.'s 50th Regiment—Captain W. Knowles, leg amputated, dangerously; Captain J. L. Wilton, severely wounded; Lieutenant Grimes, killed; Lieutenant H. J. Frampton, arm amputated, dangerously; Lieutenant R. B. Bellers, slightly wounded; Lieutenant W. P. Elgee, slightly wounded; Lieutenant A. White, severely wounded; Lieutenant W. Du Vernet, severely wounded; Lieutenant J. Purcell, severely wounded; Ensign W. R. Farmer, severely wounded.

48th Regiment N. Infantry—Captain Troup, slightly wounded; Captain H. Palmer, ditto; Lieutenant and Adjutant Wale, severely wounded; Ensign W. Marshall, slightly wounded.

Fourth Brigade Infantry.

36th Regiment N. Infantry—Ensign Bagshaw, wounded.

EDWARD LUGARD,
Captain, Assistant Adjutant-General.

Casualty Return of the Force under the Command of Major-General Sir H. G. Smith, K.C.B.

Camp, Aliwal, January 29, 1846.

Artillery—3 men, 30 horses, killed; 15 men, 9 horses, wounded; 5 men, 12 horses, missing.

Cavalry.
First Brigade.

H. M.'s 16th Lancers—2 European officers, 56 men, 77 horses, killed; 6 European officers, 77 men, 22 horses, wounded; 1 man, 73 horses, missing.

3rd Light Cavalry—2 native officers, 27 men, 42 horses, killed; 1 native officer, 21 men, 7 horses, wounded.

4th Irregular Cavalry—1 European officer, 1 horse, killed; 2 men, 3 horses, wounded.

Total—3 European officers, 2 native officers, 83 men, 120 horses, killed; 6 European officers, 1 native officer, 100 men, 32 horses, wounded; 1 man, 73 horses, missing.

Second Brigade.

Governor-General's Body-Guard—1 horse killed; 4 horses wounded; 3 horses missing.

1st Light Cavalry—9 men, 19 horses, killed; 2 European officers, 14 men, 9 horses, wounded; 4 horses missing.

5th Light Cavalry—1 man, 3 horses, killed; 1 native officer, 8 men, 10 horses, wounded; 4 horses missing.

Shekawattee Cavalry—1 man, 2 horses, killed; 2 native officers, 12 men, 15 horses, wounded; 1 horse missing.

Total—11 men, 25 horses, killed; 2 European officers, 3 native officers, 34 men, 38 horses, wounded; 12 horses missing.

Infantry.
First Brigade.

H. M.'s 31st Regiment—1 man killed; 1 European officer, 14 men, wounded.

24th Native Infantry—1 European officer, 5 men, wounded; 7 men missing.

47th Native Infantry—1 man killed; 9 men wounded.

    Total—2 men killed; 2 European officers, 28 men, wounded; 7 men missing.

Second Brigade.

H. M.'s 50th Regiment—1 European officer, 9 men, killed; 10 European officers, 59 men, wounded; 4 men missing.

48th Native Infantry—1 native officer, 9 men, 1 horse, killed; 4 European officers, 1 native officer, 36 men, wounded.

Sirmoor Battalion—9 men, 1 horse, killed; 1 native officer, 39 men, wounded.

    Total—1 European officer, 1 native officer, 27 men, 2 horses, killed; 14 European officers, 2 native officers, 134 men, wounded; 4 men missing.

Third Brigade.

H. M.'s 53rd Regiment—3 men killed; 8 men wounded; 2 men missing.

30th Native Infantry—4 men killed; 24 men wounded; 1 man missing.

    Total—7 men killed; 32 men wounded; 3 men missing.

Fourth Brigade.

36th Native Infantry—3 men killed; 1 European officer, 10 men, wounded; 1 man missing.

Nusseeree Battalion—6 men killed; 16 men wounded.

    Total—9 men killed; 1 European officer, 26 men, wounded; 1 man missing.

Shekawattee Infantry—2 men killed; 13 men wounded; 4 men missing.

Sappers and Miners—None killed or wounded.

    Total killed—151 men, 177 horses; total wounded—413 men, 79 horses; total missing—25 men, 97 horses.

    Grand total of killed, wounded, and missing—589 men.

    Grand total of killed, wounded, and missing—353 horses.

                        H. G. SMITH, Major-General.

Return of Ordnance captured from the Enemy, in Action at Aliwal, by the 1st Division of the Army of the Sutlej, under the personal Command of Major-General Sir Harry Smith, K.C.B., on the 28th January, 1846.

Camp, Aliwal, 30th January, 1846.

Howitzers.

One brass 8-inch, 2 feet 9 inches long, serviceable.
One brass 24-pounder, 3 feet 11 inches long, serviceable.
One copper 13-pounder, 3 feet 9 inches long, serviceable.
One brass 12-pounder, 4 feet 9 inches long, serviceable.
One brass 12-pounder, 4 feet 9 inches long, serviceable.
One brass 7-pounder, 3 feet 5½ inches long, unserviceable.
One copper 12-pounder, 3 feet 9 inches long, serviceable.
One copper 12-pounder, 3 feet 9 inches long, serviceable.
One copper 12-pounder, 3 feet 9 inches long, serviceable.
One brass 12-pounder, 3 feet 9 inches long, highly ornamented, serviceable.
One copper 9-pounder, 3 feet 11 inches long, highly ornamented, carriage inlaid with brass and steel, serviceable.
One copper 9-pounder, 2 feet 9½ inches long, serviceable.
One copper 12-pounder, 3 feet 4½ inches long, serviceable.

Mortars.

One brass 10-inch, 2 feet 3 inches long, mounted on a field carriage, serviceable.
One copper 8¼-inch, 1 foot 9 inches long, mounted on a field carriage, serviceable.
One brass 6-inch, 1 foot 4½ inches long, a curious old piece, with highly carved and ornamented carriage, mounted on a field carriage.
One brass 4½-inch, 1 foot 4¼ inches long, a curious old piece, mounted on a field carriage.

Guns.

One brass 8-pounder, 10 feet 2 inches long, ornamented with dolphins and rings, apparently a French battering gun, being heavy metal, serviceable.

One copper 8-pounder, 4 feet 11¾ inches long, serviceable.
One brass 8-pounder, 4 feet 11 inches long, serviceable.
One brass 8-pounder, 5 feet 1 inch long, serviceable.
One brass 7-pounder, 4 feet 11 inches long, heavy metal, serviceable.
One brass 7-pounder, 4 feet 3½ inches long, heavy metal, serviceable.
One copper 6½-pounder, 5 feet 1 inch long, serviceable.
One brass 6-pounder, 5 feet long, serviceable.
One brass 6-pounder, 4 feet 1 inch long, serviceable.
One copper 6-pounder, 5 feet 3½ inches long, serviceable.
One brass 6-pounder, 5 feet 5½ inches long, unserviceable, being heavy metal.
One brass 6-pounder, 4 feet 11 inches long, serviceable, being heavy metal.
One 6-pounder, 4 feet 10½ inches long, inscription in English characters, owner, King Runjeet Sing, Commander Meg Sing, Kawkur, maker Rai Sing, Lahore, 1833, No. 1, serviceable.
One 6-pounder, 4 feet 8 inches long, serviceable.
One 6-pounder, 4 feet 11½ inches long, highly ornamented carriage, serviceable.
One 6-pounder, 4 feet 11 inches long, inscription in English characters, owner King Runjeet Sing, Commander Meg Sing, Kawkur, maker Rai Sing, Lahore, 1833, No. 1, serviceable.
One 6-pounder, 4 feet 8 inches, Persian inscription, serviceable.
One 6-pounder, 5 feet long, no inscription, serviceable,
One copper 6-pounder, 5 feet long, no inscription, serviceable.
One brass 6-pounder, 4 feet 10½ inches long, no inscription, serviceable.
One 6-pounder, 4 feet 10½ inches long, no inscription, serviceable.
One copper 6-pounder, 4 feet 11 inches long, being highly ornamented, carriage inlaid with brass and steel, serviceable.

One 6-pounder, 4 feet 11 inches long, being highly ornamented, carriage inlaid with brass and steel, serviceable.

One brass 6-pounder, 4 feet 11 inches long, no inscription, serviceable.

One brass 6-pounder, 4 feet $9\frac{1}{2}$ inches long, no inscription, serviceable.

One copper 6-pounder, 4 feet $10\frac{3}{4}$ inches long, no inscription, serviceable.

One gun-metal 6-pounder, 4 feet $10\frac{1}{2}$ inches long, no inscription, apparently a capital gun.

One brass $5\frac{3}{4}$-pounder, 5 feet 7 inches long, Persian inscription, serviceable.

One brass $5\frac{3}{4}$ pounder, 5 feet 9 inches long, no inscription, being heavy metal.

One brass 4-pounder, 4 feet 7 inches long, no inscription, being heavy metal, serviceable.

One copper 3-pounder, 3 feet long, Persian inscription, serviceable.

One $3\frac{1}{2}$-inch brass pounder, 4 feet 7 inches long, no inscription, serviceable, being heavy metal.

One unknown, sunk in Sutlej.

One unknown, sunk in Sutlej.

One unknown, sunk in Sutlej.

One unknown, sunk in Sutlej.

One unknown, spiked on the opposite bank.

One unknown, spiked on the opposite bank.

One brass 6-pounder, taken possession of in the fort of Gungrana.

One 9-pounder, no inscription, taken possession of in the fort of Gungrana.

One 6-pounder, 4 feet 11 inches long, no inscription, serviceable.

Seven, unknown, sunk in the Sutlej.

Two guns, since brought in, unknown.

Abstract of Captured Ordnance.

Serviceable—12 howitzers, 4 mortars, 33 guns; total, 49.
Unserviceable—1 howitzer, 2 guns; total 3.
Sunk in the Sutlej, and spiked on the opposite shore—13 guns.
Since brought in—2 guns.
  Grand total, 67.

Forty swivel camel-guns also captured, which have been destroyed.

G. LAWRENSON,
Major, 2nd Brigade Horse Artillery, Commanding Artillery,
1st Division, Army of the Sutlej.

N.B.—The quantity of ammunition captured with the artillery, and found in the camp of the enemy, is beyond accurate calculation, consisting of shot, shell, grape, and small arm ammunition of every description, and for every calibre. The powder found in the limbers and waggons of the guns and in the magazines of the intrenched camp has been destroyed, to prevent accidents. Six large hackery-loads have also been appropriated to the destruction of forts in the neighbourhood. As many of the shot and shell as time would admit of being collected, have been brought into the park—the shells, being useless, have been thrown into the river. The shot will be appropriated to the public service.

G. LAWRENSON,
Major, 2nd Brigade Horse Artillery, Commanding Artillery,
1st Division, Army of the Sutlej.

Chapter 7
The Battle of Sobraon

Sergeant Pearman of the 3rd Light Dragoons on the march to Sobraon

At last we got orders to join the main army at Sobraon under command of Sir Hugh Gough. The camp was a very large camp.

It lay in almost a line in echelon of regiments and was twenty-seven miles in length—about 43,000 men. The 9th Queen's Lancers were at the right. The distance between was filled up with infantry and artillery and cavalry, native and European. The enemy lay on the banks of the Sutlej river in an entrenched camp with about 120 guns and 70,000 fighting men. We arrived in camp with the 16th Lancers, as we got our food with that regiment, but still rode the horses of Colonel Alexander's Troop of Bengal Horse Artillery.

****

From Sir Harry Smith's Autobiography

I marched on the morning of the 3rd February on my route back to the Commander-in-Chief.

I had with me three troops of Horse Artillery, two 8-inch howitzers, the 16th Lancers, the 3rd and 5th Light Cavalry, one corps of Irregular Horse, H.M.'s 31st, 50th, and 53rd Regiments, and 200 convalescents, and of Native

Infantry the 47th Regiment, and the Sermoor and Nusseeree Battalions. The rest of my Aliwal heroes remained with Wheeler.

I reached the right of the army on the 7th, and was received by the Commander-in-Chief with a burst of enthusiastic welcome to be equalled only by that of the army at large. His Excellency addressed each Corps in terms as gratifying to them as to me, and I, Staff, Commanding Officers of Corps, Prince Waldemar, etc., dined with the Commander-in-Chief, who again, in a speech when drinking our health, bestowed upon us every encomium, and attached the utmost importance to the great cause—our signal victory. The Governor-General was at Ferozepore.

The ground I had been directed to occupy being filthy to excess, I begged to move my position, which I was permitted to do on the 8th. On this day the Governor-General arrived in camp. He sent for me, and received me with all the warmth of a long-standing friendship, and bestowed personally upon me all the praises he had so lavishly given me in his General Orders.

On the 9th, all Generals of Divisions, Brigadiers, and Heads of Departments were summoned in the afternoon to attend in the Commander-in-Chief's tent. I pretty clearly guessed the purport of such a summons. His Excellency explained to all that the enemy's most strongly fortified position was to be attacked at daylight, and he clearly detailed to each General and Commander his position and portion of the attack.

In my own mind I very much disagreed with my gallant Commander-in-Chief as to the place of his attack being the most eligible one. I saw at once that the fundamental principle of 'being superior to your enemy on the point of attack' was lost sight of, and the whole of our army, with the exception of my Division, which was reduced to 2400 bayonets, was held in reserve just out of the reach of the enemy's cannon.

At daylight our heavy guns (which had been placed with the object of destroying or greatly impairing the enemy's defences) opened fire, and with apparent success where the fire was the most heavy, but to our astonishment, at the very moment of this success our fire slackened and soon ceased altogether, when it was ascertained that the ammunition was expended, the officer in command of the Artillery not having brought half the quota into the field which was ordered by the Governor-General and the Commander-in-Chief. Thus no time was to be lost.

****

(At this point Sir Harry Smith's autobiography ends. He laid down his pen, probably through temporary illness, and never took it up again. In place of any fuller account of the battle of Sobraon, we have only passages from two letters, included below, relating to his share in the victory.)

****

An account by Ensign Newall
who was with the Artillery

Had the morning been clear it would have been serious for us, but the same veil of heavy mist which so hampered us hung over the hostile camp, and concealed from the view of the enemy the formidable peak of heavy cannon being aligned on the prolongation of his bastion faces and flanks. On that day, when I first smelt powder, I served with the heavy howitzers and can never forget the moment when old Gough (who was there present in person) sent the order to "open fire." No 1 fire! No 2, 3, 4, 5, 6. Six 10-inch shells hurtled through the mist just lifting, and could be seen in the still dark morning light, bursting in the enemy's camp and entrenchments. A minute's pause, and then the hum of the surprised camp like a vast hive, followed by the drums beating to arms, and the trumpets of the Sikh hosts sounding the alarm.

****

Sergeant Pearman of the 3rd Light Dragoons on the Battle of Sobraon

From 7 a.m. until about 12 noon, firing was maintained, the round shot bounding playfully and spitefully over the plain. At about 10 a.m. all the troops for the attack had been collected in their brigades, and the brigades were united in their several divisions.

The order was now given to advance, and General Gilbert's Division, in the centre, threw out skirmishers to attack the enemy from the right and left. The whole was now moving slowly to the entrenchments, so as to enter them by an assault, as soon as General Dick, on the left, and Smith, on the right, had gained an entrance. I saw Abercrombie's sappers making a lodgement on the works, but not before the 50th Foot and 62nd and 80th and 10th Regiments of H. Majesty had been once turned back from the batteries and again taken up the charge. Oh, what a sight to sit on your horse and look at these brave fellows as they tried several times to get into the enemy's camp; and at last they did, but oh, what a loss of human life. God only knows who will have to answer for it.

After this the infantry got some cover until the Sikhs had been driven out from the entrenchments. The 1st European Bengal Regiment did good service, and a regiment of Ghurkhas with them—a brave mountain race. Our regiment, the 3rd Light Dragoons being in the centre we could see a great deal of the field. Such a tearing and rending of the atmosphere has never been heard before in this country.

The 31st Foot at the battle of Sobraon

After we had gained a lodgement, the firing slackened a little, and ours did likewise, and now comes the time of strife. Orders came for all the regiments— (regiments had been lying down for a long time)—to stand to arms. General Gilbert now threw out his Light Infantry, the whole about a hundred yards to the front, to make the demonstration of attack, while on the right and left the whole of General Dick's and General Smith's divisions moved to the front. The horse artillery of Dick's division cantered to the front some few hundred yards and poured in a tremendous discharge of grape. The infantry coming up in the line opened a musketry fire when within an easy distance, and Sir Harry Smith's the same. Oh, what a thunder!

General Gilbert's division was now advancing from the centre, which was taken up by the other division, and forward the long line of infantry went, two deep, for several miles in length. The enemy's shot now came on amongst the men, and it seemed difficult to fill up the gaps made; but on they go: British troops are not to be deterred. But no one could expect to escape such a fire. The enemy was now pouring in their grape at point blank range. Our artillery closed up to quarter distance, followed by the 3rd Light Dragoons, my regiment.

The advance of the army was now changed from line to echelon, and now the troops advanced. It was about 11 o'clock a.m. General Dick's division had reached the entrenchments and was fighting like mad. A rush was made forward by the 1st regiment of Europeans with a shout, the Ghurkhas close with them. The Ghurkhas are dressed in dark green. They kept time and pace with our English regiments. The Sikhs were fighting bravely for their guns and camp, and our men meant to have them, and have them they did. But, oh, to tell the loss! The 1st Bengal Europeans had but 167 men on parade next morning—the remains of a noble regiment.

The Sikhs now began to retreat, but gave us parting shots as they left the parapets of the entrenchments. The Colours of two English regiments were now planted on the batteries. The enemy now formed themselves in strong close battalions to make good their retreat to the bridge of boats across the river Sutlej behind their camp.

It was now our turn. It was given: 'Forward, 3rd King's Own Light Dragoons', an order the Colonel used when he was in a good temper. On we went by the dead and dying, and partly over the poor fellows, and up the parapet our horses scrambled. One of the Sikh artillery men struck at me with his sponge staff but missed me, hitting my horse on the hindquarters, which made the horse bend down. I cut a round cut at him and felt my sword strike him but could not say where, there was such a smoke on. I went with the rest through the camp at their battalions which we broke up.

****

FROM HARRY SMITH'S LETTER TO
HIS SISTER MRS. SARGANT

Camp Lahore, 25th February, 1846
Our last fight was an awful one. My reduced-in-numbers Division—only 2400 bayonets—was, as in other fights, placed in reserve, but pretty soon brought into action, and as at Ferozeshuhur again I had the good luck to turn the fortune of the day. In so doing I lost out of my 2400 men, 635 killed and wounded. My first attack on the entrenchments was repulsed. I attacked when I did not wish, and

had to take ground close to the river on the enemy's left, consequently our right. By dint of the hardest fighting I ever saw (except Badajoz, New Orleans, and Waterloo) I carried the entrenchments. By Jupiter! the enemy were within a hair's-breadth of driving me back. Their numbers exceeded mine. And such a hand-to-hand conflict ensued, for 25 minutes I could barely hold my own.

Mixed together, swords and targets against bayonets, and a fire on both sides. I never was in such a personal fight for half the time, but my bulldogs of the 31st and old 50th stood up like men, were well supported by the native regiments, and my position closed the fight which staggered everywhere. Then such a scene of shooting men fording a deep river, as no one I believe ever saw before. The bodies made a bridge, but the fire of our musketry and cannon killed everyone who rushed.

The hand of Almighty God has been upon me, for I may say to you what all the army knows, I was foremost in the fight, and on a noble horse the whole time, which sprang over the enemy's works like a deer, neither he nor I nor my clothes being scratched. It is a miracle for which I am, I trust, even more grateful to my God than humble towards my comrades.

You always so desired I should distinguish myself. I have now gratified you, although I so egotistically write it to my sister, and in every battle have I with my noble horses been exposed without a graze. The only thing was my stick shot out of my hand; my clothes are covered with blood in many cases. Poor Holdich got a bad wound in the shoulder and arm. He is a gallant and cool boy as ever lived. He is at Ferozepore, too far off for me to go and see, or I should do so and write to his mother.

****

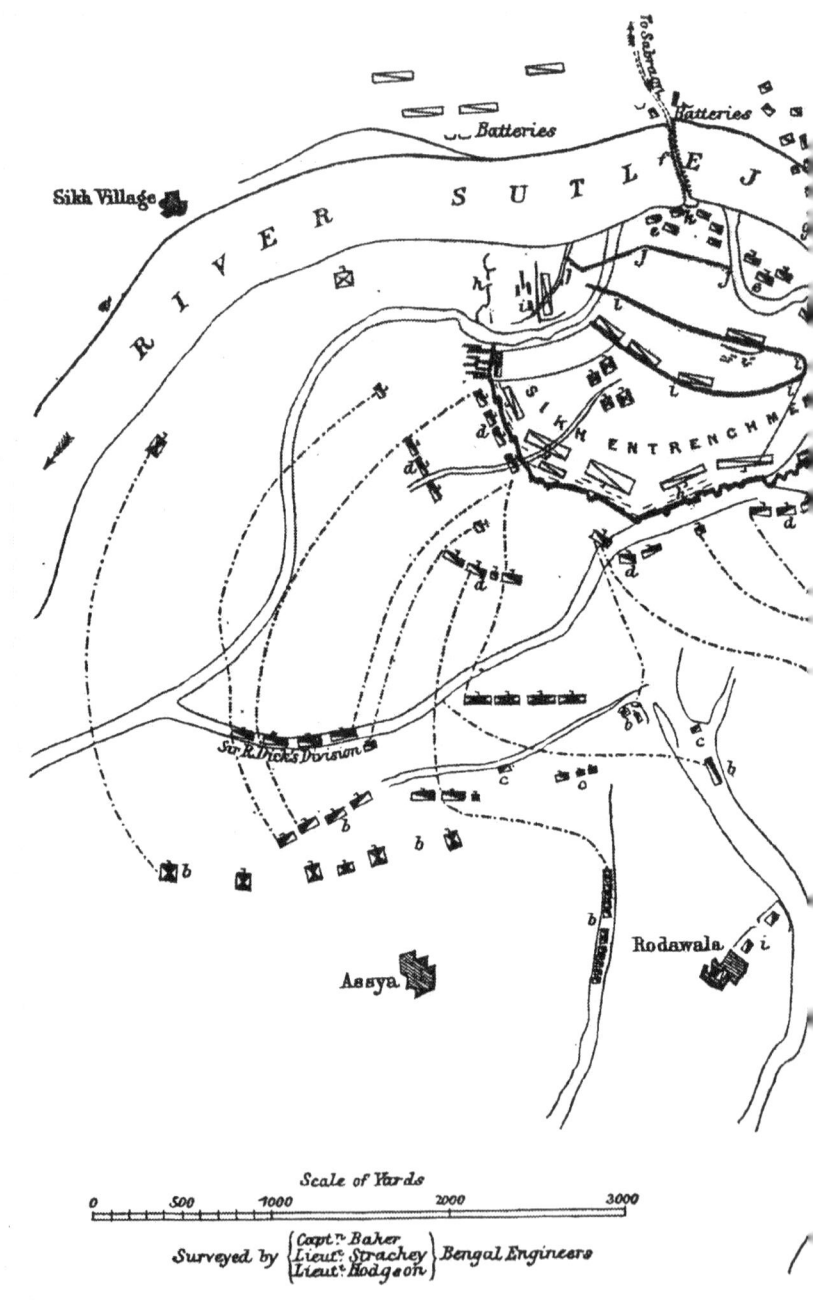

THE BATTLE OF SOBRAON—FEBRUARY 10TH, 1846

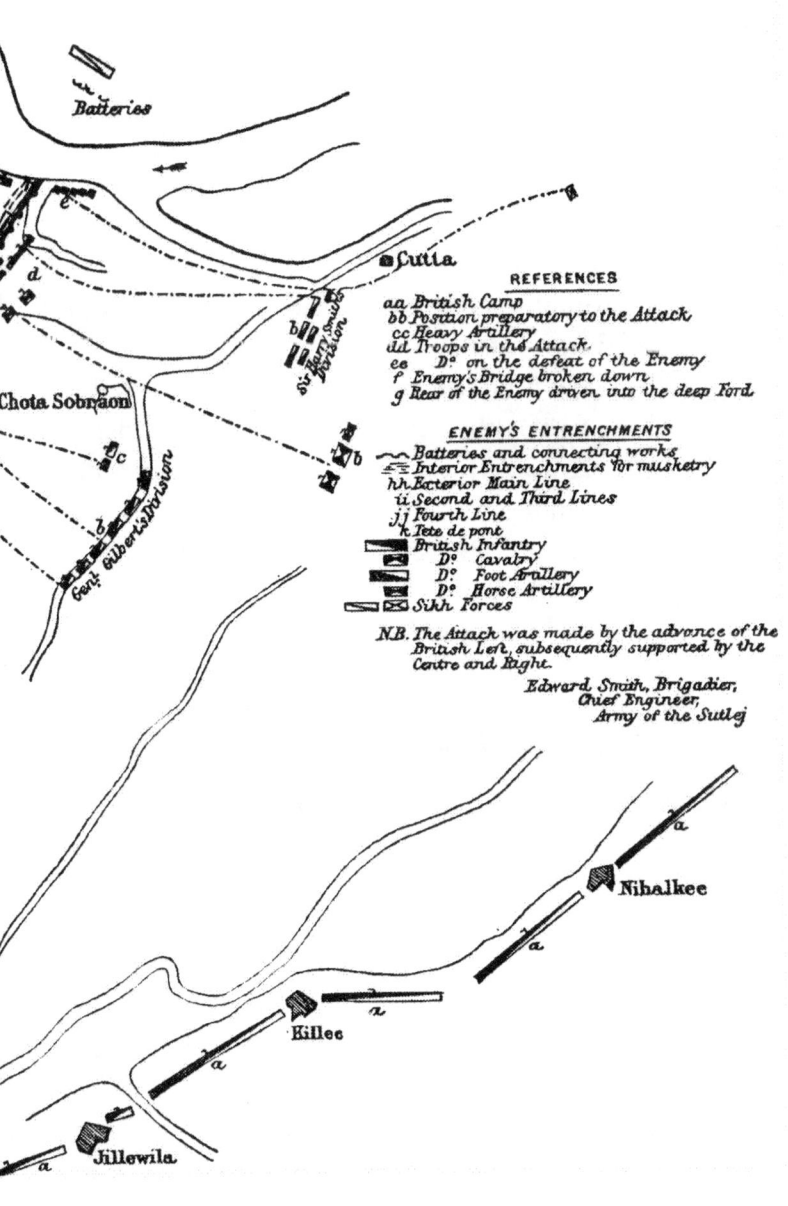

From Hary Smith's letter to Sir James Kempt

24th February, 1846

I never was in such a hand-to-hand fight; my gallant 31st and 50th literally staggered under the war of cannon and musketry. Behind such formidable entrenchments I could not get in where I was ordered to attack, but had to turn my right close to the river, where, if left alone, I should have commenced. I carried the works by dint of English pluck, although the native corps stuck close to me, and when I got in, such hand-to-hand work I have never witnessed. For twenty-five minutes we were at it against four times my numbers, sometimes receding (never turning round, though), sometimes advancing.

The old 31st and 50th laid on like devils.... This last was a brutal bulldog fight, although of vast political and definite results; but my fight at Aliwal was a little sweeping second edition of Salamanca—a stand-up gentlemanlike battle, a mixing of all arms and laying-on, carrying everything before us by weight of attack and combination, all hands at work from one end of the field to the other.

****

Private Baldwin of H.M. 9th Regiment of Foot on the Battle of Sobraon

On February 9th, 1846, at night, we received orders to prepare for action next morning, which caused a general excitement among our troops. Artillery, Cavalry, and Infantry were all in a state of exhilaration, taking up the most advantageous positions. Early in the morning, before the enemy's picket withdrew, a regiment of Ghoorkahs, in our service, took them by surprise, and destroyed the whole of them with their choorahs. It seems that they (the enemy's picket) were not watching with vigilance, as was their duty, but were sleeping, though probably not dreaming of their fearful end.

These Ghoorkahs are a very diminutive race of men, but decidedly the best Day and Martin soldiers in India, boasting they are an arm's length better soldiers than any other native tribes in the country, and that we are the same length better than they. We celebrated the anniversary of Her Gracious Majesty's wedding day (February 10th) by firing a feu de joie. At the dawn of day having every thing definitely arranged to give battle, our Artillery poured a volley of shells and rockets into the enemy's camp, arousing them from their slumber, and on their not retaliating, we thought they were decamping; but soon, however, they got their guns to bear upon us, though happily their aim was bad, for most part of their shells burst in the air, and the long shots all bounded over the ravines in which we (Infantry) were sheltered.

We now made the Seikhs feel the full weight of our wrath; our rockets in particular did great execution, spreading fearful terror and destruction amongst them. After some splendid cannonading for about three hours, the Infantry advanced, when our regiment, being in the rear, forming the reserve, we had a very beautiful view of the attack; what a magnificent sight to be sure! I shall never forget it.

Her Majesty's 10th regiment was in front of us, and most of their men threw aside their heavy shakos (caps) and went in a perisher! (as we term it) with the Seikhs; it was quite a novelty to them as their regiment was never before engaged in battle; they came to close quarters and were repulsed, but when they saw our brigade advancing, they renewed the attack and drove back the enemy, but not without a great sacrifice of men, for the slaughter here was terrible.

It was there Sir Robert Dick was killed, a brave veteran and Waterloo officer, whose loss was deeply lamented by all his regiment.

At another part of the camp Her Majesty's 29th was repulsed three times, and the enemy's Cavalry charged them, and out off 29 men's heads, before our horsemen could get to their assistance; we afterwards placed the bodies in a row, and remarked that it was singular enough, the number of the regiment should exactly correspond with the 29 decapitated fellows who lay before us. The 3rd Dragoons here made a brilliant charge, while we were advancing, and chopped the Seikhs down at a tremendous rate.

In a foregoing page I mentioned Lieutenant Creagh; as our brigade was advancing in line towards the scene of action, this officer in charge of my company was marching in the ordinary manner, a man on either side of him, when instinctively he suddenly bowed himself down and the next moment a cannon ball passed right over him, and went smashing through a drum head which a boy was carrying. Had this not been the case at the moment, he would certainly have been struck in the chest.

While advancing we were all at once alarmed at seeing in front of us, to the right, one of our ammunition waggons in a blaze, and the poor frightened horses urged on by the fierce flame behind them, galloping in full speed towards the enemy's camp, the battle at the same time raging on all sides.

I think it was about nine o'clock that our Artillery ceased firing, then we (Infantry) and all the Cavalry attacked the Seikhs with bright steel, which they cannot stand; we slaughtered thousands in the camp, and thousands that escaped the sword and bayonet, were either shot or drowned while crossing the river Sutlej, as their bridge had been previously destroyed by our Artillery's fire. There was a battery of guns on the other side of the river, which made great havoc in our ranks, and these the enemy bore away in their flight.

We were an equal match for the foe at Sobraon, having our army reinforced, whilst theirs was reduced; notwithstanding, they then had the superiority, besides the advantage of an entrenched camp, defended by about 36,000 men and 70 bulldogs; (great guns) and having a double row of half-moon batteries—high ramparts, with immense deep and wide ditches—a triple line of defences of earth and planks, with facines, redoubts, and epaulments.

You see the camp was as inaccessible as a formidable fort; the Seikhs were determined we should not run in upon them and take their guns this time without great difficulty. The battle was nearly over when our brigade entered their camp at one end, and got in the rear of their strongest position, but we found ourselves between two fires—from a battery on the other side of the Sutlej on our left, and from the remnant of their Infantry and Artillery on the right; but happily for us their exertions had little or no effect. Soon the enemy yielded, offering no further resistance, and I really could not help feeling for their Infantry, at seeing them marching away so deliberately with trailed arms—offering no return whatever to our galling fire; and as they got out of our reach, fell victims to our more advanced troops, which extended as far as the river's bank.

You have, doubtless, read of the "red sea;" and the

Sutlej now might very well be called the "red river" from the blood of thousands of the Seikhs, many of whose bodies are floating down the river at this time.

****

Major W. S. R Hodson of the 1st Bengal European Fusiliers on the Battle of Sobraon

We have been knocked about for some days so incessantly that there has been no chance of writing anything; and even this scrawl, I fear, will hardly reach you. You will hear publicly of our great victory of the 10th, and of the total and final rout of the Sikh force. But first, I must tell you that the 2nd Grenadiers were sent back about a week ago to the villages and posts in our rear, to keep open the communication. At Sobraon.

Not liking the notion of returning to the rear while an enemy was in front, I applied immediately to do duty with another regiment; my petition was granted; and I joined the 16th Grenadiers on the evening of the 9th inst. About three in the morning we advanced towards the Sikh entrenchments along the river's bank. Our guns and ammunition had all come up a day or two before, and during the night were placed in position to shell their camp.

At daybreak, seventeen heavy mortars and howitzers, rockets, and heavy guns commenced a magnificent fire on their position; at half-past eight the infantry advanced, Sir R. Dick's division on the right, and ours (Gilbert's) in front, covered by our fire from the batteries.

On we went as usual in the teeth of a dreadful fire of guns and musketry, and after a desperate struggle we got within their triple and quadruple entrenchments; and then their day of reckoning came indeed. Driven

Major J. Smyth of the 16th Lancers

from trench to trench, and surrounded on all sides, they retired, fighting most bravely, to the river, into which they were driven pell-mell, a tremendous fire of musketry pouring on them from our bank, and the Horse Artillery finishing their destruction with grape.

The river is literally choked with corpses, and their camp full of dead and dying. An intercepted letter of theirs shows that they have lost 20,000 in killed, wounded, and missing; all their guns remaining in our hands. I had the pleasure myself of spiking two guns which were turned on us. Once more I have escaped, I am thankful to say, unhurt, except that a bullet took a fancy to my little finger and cut the skin off the top of it, a mere pin scratch, though it spoiled a buckskin glove.

****

ENSIGN PERCY INNES OF THE BENGAL EUROPEAN REGIMENT WRITES ABOUT SUFFERING ARTILLERY AT SOBRAON

The air, charged with sulphur, was stifling and so heated that it was almost unbearable. Now on rushed the Bengal European Regiment with a determination which promised to carry everything before it; soon reaching the ditch which formed the outer defence, and springing into it, they found themselves confronted by the massive walls, which in the distance had appeared less formidable, for they now found these works too high to escalade without ladders. To retire again was to encounter the storm of fire through which they had just passed, to remain in their present position was annihilation; therefore, the Regiment, mortified and chagrined, was forced to seek shelter under cover of the bank of the dry river which it had left but a short time before.

****

A description by the Governor-General's son, Arthur Hardinge, of the Sikh attempt to flee across the river

I saw the bridge at that moment overcrowded with guns, horses, and soldiers of all arms, swaying to and fro, till at last with a crash it disappeared in the running waters, carrying with it all those who had vainly hoped to reach the opposite shore. The river seemed alive with a struggling mass of men. The artillery, now brought down to the water's edge, completed the slaughter. Few escaped; none, it may be said, surrendered.

****

Captain Cunningham on the last defence of the Sikhs

Calling on all around to fight for the Guru, who had promised everlasting bliss to the brave, he repeatedly rallied his shattered ranks, and at last fell a martyr on a heap of his slain countrymen. Others might be seen standing on the ramparts and amid a shower of balls, waving defiance with their swords, or telling the gunners where the fair-haired English pressed thickest together . . . . The parapets were sprinkled with blood from end to end; the trenches were filled with the dead and the dying. Amid the deafening roar of cannon, and the multitudinous fire of musketry, shouts of triumph or of scorn were yet heard, and the flashing of innumerable swords was yet visible; or from time to time exploding magazines of powder threw bursting shells and beams of wood and banks of earth high above the agitated sea of smoke and flame which enveloped the host of combatants . . . .

****

Sergeant Pearman of the 3rd Light Dragoons on the end of the Battle of Sobraon

Our regiment at this time was not 300 strong out of 700 that took the field on December 12th, 1845, and this was February 10th, 1846. In this charge we lost twenty-three men, four of them out of my tent, but two of them, it was their own fault: Jack Marshall who had been drinking for several days. I was told he went out after the fighting was nearly over to attack a Sikh on horseback. His comrade, Bill Driver, a fine young man, six feet high, seeing that he was likely to get the worse of it (as we all could see), trotted out to his assistance. Just as he got to Marshall, who was just killed, a shot came and struck poor Bill. He threw up his arms, and down he came, his horse coming back to the regiment, when we caught it.

The enemy was now rushing to the ford, as the bridge was broken and on fire and being choked up with a mass of soldiers, camels and horses with some artillery and carriages. Some of the boats got loose, the river being rapid at the time. The whole, mass was turned into the river. From what we were told it was believed that about 10,000 souls perished in ten minutes or a quarter of an hour. Sir Harry Smith's division came up by the river bank and killed thousands of the enemy while they endeavoured to cross the river.

We now possessed the entrenchments and camp, taking all their guns, nearly one hundred in all. The dead Sikh bodies that lay at their guns and at the parapets! They certainly were a brave enemy, and I must say that their retreat from the camp to the river was as steady as could be, although we charged and the artillery raked them wherever they were able, to say nothing of our infantry with shot and bayonet. There were heaps of dead beside those who were drowned in the river. These were all their regular or Aeen Battalions. None of our army crossed to the other side of the river—we had done enough. The Battle of Sobraon, the most severely contested of any one in the campaign, was over and our victory complete, but had the 9th Lancers and their Cavalry Brigade been on the other side, not a man of the 70,000 would have been left.

****

FROM GENERAL SIR HUGH GOUGH'S REPORT OF FEBRUARY 13TH, 1846, ON THE BATTLE OF SOBRAON, TO LORD HARDINGE, THE GOVERNOR-GENERAL OF INDIA

This is the fourth despatch which I have had the honour of addressing to you since the opening of the campaign. My last communication detailed the movements of the Sikhs and our counter-manoeuvres since the great day of Ferozeshah.

Defeated on the Upper Sutlej, the enemy continued to occupy his position on the right bank, and his formidable tête de pout and entrenchments on the left bank of the river, in front of the main body of our army. But. on the 10th instant, all that he held of British territory, which was comprised in the ground on which one of his camps stood, was stormed from his grasp, and his audacity was again signally punished by a blow, sudden, heavy, and overwhelming. It is my gratifying duty to detail the measures which have led to this glorious result.

The enemy's works had been repeatedly reconnoitred during the time of my headquarters being fixed at Nihalkee, by myself, my departmental staff, and my engineer and artillery officers. Our observations, coupled with the reports of spies, convinced us that there had devolved on us the arduous task of attacking a position covered with formidable entrenchments, not fewer than 30,000 men, the best of the Khalsa troops, with seventy pieces of cannon, united by a good bridge to a reserve on the opposite bank, on which the enemy had a considerable camp and some artillery, commanding and flanking his field-works on our side.

Major-General Sir Harry Smith's division having rejoined me on the evening of the 8th, and part of my siege-train having come up with me, I resolved, on the morning of the 10th to dispose our mortars and battering guns on the alluvial land within good range of the enemy's works. To enable us to do this, it was necessary first to drive in the enemy's piquets at the post of observation in front of Kodeewalla, and at the Little Sobraon. It was directed that this should be done during the night of the 9th, but the execution of this part of the plan was deferred, owing to misconceptions and casual circumstances, until near daybreak.

The delay was of little importance, as the event showed that the Sikhs had followed our example, in occupying the two posts in force by day only. Of both, therefore, possession was taken without opposition. The battering and disposable field-artillery was then put in position on an extended semicircle, embracing within its fire the works of the Sikhs. It had been intended that the cannonade should have commenced at daybreak; but so heavy a mist hung over the plain and river, that it became necessary to wait until the rays of the sun had penetrated it and cleared the atmosphere. Meanwhile, on the margin of the Sutlej, on our left, two brigades of Major-General Sir Robert Dick's division, under his personal command, stood ready to commence the assault against the enemy's extreme right. His 7th brigade, in which was the 10th foot, reinforced by the 53rd foot, and led by Brigadier Stacy, was to head the attack, supported at 200 yards' distance by the 6th brigade, under Brigadier Wilkinson.

In reserve was the 5th brigade, under Brigadier the Honourable T. Ashburnham, which was to move forward from the entrenched village of Kodeewalla, leaving, if necessary, a regiment for its defence. In the centre, Major-General Gilbert's division was deployed for support or attack, its right resting on and in the village of the Little Sobraon. Major-General Sir Harry Smith's division was formed near the village of Guttah, with its right thrown up towards the Sutlej. Brigadier Cureton's cavalry threatened, by feigned attacks, the ford at Hurrekee and the enemy's horse, under Raja Lall Sing Misr, on the opposite bank. Brigadier Campbell, taking an intermediate position in the rear between Major-General Gilbert's right and Major-General Sir Harry Smith's left, protected both. Major-General Sir Joseph Thackwell, under whom was Brigadier Scott, held in reserve on our left, ready to act as circumstances might demand, the rest of the cavalry.

Our battery of nine-pounders, enlarged into twelves, opened near the Little Sobraon with a brigade of howitzers formed from the light field-batteries and troops of horse artillery, shortly after daybreak. But it was half-past six before the whole of our artillery fire was developed. It was most spirited and well directed. I cannot speak in terms too high of the judicious disposition of the guns, their admirable practice, or the activity with which the cannonade was sustained. But, notwithstanding the formidable calibre of our iron guns, mortars, and howitzers, and the admirable way in which they were served, and aided by a rocket battery, it would have been visionary to expect that they could, within any limited time, silence the fire of seventy pieces behind well constructed batteries of earth, plank, and fascines, or dislodge troops, covered either by redoubts or epaulments, or within a treble line of trenches.

The effect of the cannonade was, as has been since proved by an inspection of the camp, most severely felt by the enemy; but it soon became evident that the issue of this struggle must be brought to the arbitrament of musketry and bayonet.

At nine o'clock, Brigadier Stacy's brigade, supported on either flank by Captains Horsford's and Fordyce's batteries, and Lieutenant-Colonel Lane's troop of horse artillery, moved to the attack in admirable order. The infantry and guns aided each other correlatively. The former marched steadily on in line, which they halted only to correct when necessary. The latter took up successive positions at the gallop, until at length they were within 300 yards of the heavy batteries of the Sikhs; but, notwithstanding the regularity and coolness, and scientific character of this assault, which Brigadier Wilkinson well supported, so hot was the fire of cannon, musketry, and zumboorucks kept up by the Khalsa troops, that it seemed for some moments impossible that the entrenchments could be won under it; but soon, persevering gallantry triumphed, and the whole army had the satisfaction to see the gallant Brigadier Stacy's soldiers driving the Sikhs in confusion before them within the area of their encampment.

The 10th foot, under Lieutenant-Colonel Franks

now for the, first time brought into serious contact with the enemy, greatly distinguished themselves. This regiment never fired a shot until it had got within the works of the enemy. The onset of Her Majesty's 53rd foot was as gallant and effective. The 43rd and 59th native infantry, brigaded with them, emulated both in cool determination.

At the moment of this first success, I directed Brigadier the Honourable T. Ashburnham's brigade to move on in support; and Major-General Gilbert's and Sir Harry Smith's divisions to throw out their light troops to threaten the works, aided by artillery. As these attacks of the centre and right commenced, the fire of our heavy guns had first to be directed to the right, and then gradually to cease; but, at one time the thunder of full 120 pieces of ordnance reverberated in this mighty combat through the valley of the Sutlej; and, as it was soon seen that the weight of the whole force within the Sikh camp was likely to be thrown upon the two brigades that had passed its trenches, it became necessary to convert into close and serious attacks the demonstrations with skirmishers and artillery of the centre and right; and the battle raged with inconceivable fury from right to left.

The Sikhs, even when at particular points their entrenchments were mastered with the bayonet, strove to regain them by the fiercest conflict sword in hand. Nor was it until the cavalry of the left, under Major-General Sir Joseph Thackwell, had moved forward and ridden through the openings in the entrenchments made by our sappers, in single file, and re-formed as they passed them; and the 3rd dragoons, whom no obstacle usually held formidable by horse appears to check, had, on this day, as at Ferozeshah, galloped over and cut down the obstinate defenders of batteries and field-works, and until the full weight of three divisions of infantry, with every field artillery gun which could be sent to their aid, had been cast into the scale, that victory finally declared for the British.

The fire of the Sikhs first slackened, and then nearly ceased; and the victors, then pressing them on every side, precipitated them in masses over their bridge, and into the Sutlej, which a sudden rise of seven inches had rendered hardly fordable. In their efforts to reach the right bank through the deepened water, they suffered from our horse artillery a terrible carnage. Hundreds fell under this cannonade; hundreds upon hundreds were drowned in attempting the perilous passage. Their awful slaughter, confusion, and dismay were such as would have excited compassion in the hearts of their generous conquerors, if the Khalsa troops had not, in the earlier part of the action, sullied their gallantry by slaughtering and barbarously mangling every wounded soldier whom, in the vicissitudes of attack, the fortune of war left at their mercy.

I must pause in this narrative especially to notice the determined hardihood and bravery with which our two battalions of Ghoorkhas, the Sirmoor and Nusseeree, met the Sikhs, wherever they were opposed to them. Soldiers of small stature but indomitable spirit, they vied in ardent courage in the charge with the grenadiers of our own nation, and, armed with the short weapon of their mountains, were a terror to the Sikhs throughout this great combat.

Sixty-seven pieces of cannon, upwards of 200 camel-swivels (zumboorucks), numerous standards; and vast munitions of war, captured by our troops, are the pledges and trophies of our victory. The battle was over by eleven in the morning; and, in the forenoon, I caused our engineers to burn a part and to sink a part of the vaunted bridge of the Khalsa army, across which they had boastfully come once more to defy us, and to threaten India with ruin and devastation.

We have to deplore a loss severe in itself, but certainly not heavy when weighed in the balance against the obstacles overcome and the advantages obtained.

I have especially to lament the fall of Major-General Sir Robert Dick, K.C.B., a gallant veteran of the Peninsula and Waterloo campaigns. He survived only until evening the dangerous grape-shot wound which he received close to the enemy's entrenchments, whilst personally animating, by his dauntless example, the soldiers of Her Majesty's 80th regiment, in their career of noble daring. Major-General Gilbert, to whose gallantry and unceasing exertions I have been so deeply indebted, and whose services have been so eminent throughout this eventful campaign, and Brigadier Stacy, the leader of the brigade most hotly and successfully engaged, both received contusions. They were such as would have caused many men to retire from the field, but they did not interrupt for a moment the efforts of these heroic officers. Brigadier Maclaren, so distinguished in the campaigns in Afghanistan, at Maharajpore, and now again in our conflicts with the Sikhs, has been badly wounded by a ball in the knee. Brigadier Taylor, one of the most gallant and intelligent officers in the army, to whom I have felt deeply indebted on many occasions, fell in this fight at the head of his brigade in close encounter with the enemy, and covered with honourable wounds. Brigadier Penny, of the

Nusseeree battalion, commanding the 2nd brigade, has been wounded, but not, I trust, severely. I am deprived for the present of the valuable services of Lieutenant-Colonel J. B. Gough, C.B., acting quartermaster-general of Her Majesty's troops, whose aid I have so highly prized in all my campaigns in China and India. He received a wound from a grape shot, which is severe, but I hope not dangerous. Lient.-Colonel Barr, acting adjutant-general of Her Majesty's forces, whose superior merit as a staff officer I have before recorded, has suffered a compound fracture in the left arm by a ball. It is feared that amputation may become necessary. Lieutenant-Colonels Ryan and Petit, of the 50th foot, were both badly wounded with that gallant regiment. Captain John Fisher, commandant of the Sirmoor battalion fell at the head of his valiant little corps, respected and lamented by the whole army.

****

ROBERT CUST, A CIVILIAN, ON THE AFTERMATH OF THE BATTLE OF SOBRAON

The stream was choked with the dead and dying—the sandbanks were covered with bodies floating leisurely down; It was an awful scene, a fearful carnage. The dead Sikh lay inside his trenches—the dead European marked too distinctly the line each regiment had taken, the advance. The living Europeans remarked that nought could resist the bayonet ... As the place was -becoming dangerous from the explosion of mines. I passed out of the trenches, and rode along the dry nullah that surrounds it and marked the strong defences which the enemy had thrown up .... Our loss was heavy and the ground was here and there strewn with the slain, among whom I recognized a fine and handsome lad whom I had well known, young Hamilton, brother of Alistair Stewart. There he lay, his auburn hair weltering in his blood, his forehead fearfully gashed, his fingers cut off. Still warm, but quite dead. Flames were spreading over the Sikh camp, igniting the powder beside each gun and the air was rent with terrific explosions. The guns were now nearly all removed and our dead were being buried.

 We rode slowly home.

Afterword

The First Sikh War was over and everyone who could was riding or walking slowly home.

For those who *knew*, there was a sense of business unfinished—and so it was. The Sikhs of the Punjab had not done with the British quite yet, which made the opposite inevitable—there would be no peace until the power of the Khalsa was broken forever. Two years later there was to be another series of bloody battles, in the same theatre and against the same enemy, in which many of the same regiments and men took part.

None of this concerned Sir Harry. He had distinguished himself in the First Sikh War; and that war and Smith's role in it had had become essential building blocks in the creation of the Raj—that mighty dominion under the Queen Empress—which would rule India, a mutiny in the Bengal Army notwithstanding, as part of the greatest empire the world has ever known, for another hundred years.

The Sikhs became loyal and invaluable soldiers of the Crown, supporting the British throughout the Great Mutiny—even though their new masters had been implacable enemies only five years before the first Sepoy decided he would not bite a bullet. They remained first rate regiments in the British Indian Army through a series of small wars and two major conflicts, serving all over the world and laying down their lives in thousands—always in causes not their own except for matters of their honour.

With Indian independence, in 1947, came partition, which divided the ancestral lands of the Sikhs. The mighty kingdom of the Sikhs has gone, but at least the brave wars they fought against the British—as more than worthy foes—in the middle of the 19th century did credit to the Sikh people and nation.

For his victory at Aliwal, Sir Harry Smith was awarded the thanks of Parliament.

The speech made by the Duke of Wellington about Sir Harry's achievements was proclaimed at the time to be the warmest encomium ever given by the great man to another soldier. At that moment perhaps the Master felt the time was nigh to acknowledge one of the most able of his apprentices. We can forgive him the vanity of recognising his own guiding hand in the battle. It was a precision piece of generalship at a time when 'head on' pounding was more usual—an approach to warfare that neither Wellington nor Smith had time for. In fact, it was a term Wellington had uncharitably applied to Napoleon himself at Waterloo.

It was certain that Harry Smith would have had no problem with the Duke sharing his credit—had he needed it. Sir Harry never failed to regard his mentor as 'the greatest captain of the age' and freely admitted his debt to him for whatever military prowess he possessed. Wellington's example assuredly did not fail him, as Smith was certain it would not.

Sir Harry Smith had the distinction of Aliwal added to his baronetcy, ensuring it would be forever associated with his name. He became Sir Harry Smith, 1st Baronet of Aliwal.

Within two years of the end of the Sikh War, Sir Harry and his beloved Juana were once again back in South Africa. This time he was awarded the post of Governor of Cape Colony and High Commissioner. While there he encountered, yet again, the same problems he had faced during his first appointment, but inevitably, and in accordance with his own predictions, those problems were now made worse as a direct result of the reversal of his initiatives. Once again he had to deal with disaffected Boers and there was the perennial problem of the Kaffir tribes, particularly the Xhosa and the Khoikhoi. History tells us that he was certainly under resourced for the task he was expected to perform, but, in any event, opinion is divided as to his how effective he would have been even properly resourced.

Smith was recalled to England in 1852, but not before he had left the mark of the time he spent in the Cape marked indelibly upon its landscape. The town of Aliwal North, in the Eastern Cape, commemorates his masterpiece battle and he named another town directly after himself—Harrismith in the Free State. Whatever his vanities it is beyond doubt that Smith adored his wife always, and so he would not be disappointed that it is through her that his lasting South African connection remains. Ladysmith in Kwa Zulu-Natal achieved lasting fame—perhaps notoriety—as the location of the most memorable siege of the Boer War fought in that troubled land nearly half a century after their departure. It should serve as a reminder to Sir Harry's detractors that if he could not solve all of South Africa's problems—no one else did either!

1852 brought another momentous event. In his homeland Smith was able to attend the Waterloo Dinner at which the Duke himself presided for his veterans. It was to be the great man's last, for five months later he was dead. At the state funeral Sir Harry with a combination of enormous pride and sadness performed his final duty—as standard bearer—to the man who had been his role model and whom he admired more than any other. Smith's own hero had passed beyond—just as so many of the heroes who had marched under the sweltering sun of Spain or stood in the rain of Waterloo had passed.

Now a Lieutenant-General, Harry Smith served as a soldier through several garrison commands. Then, in 1860, eight years after the death of the Duke of Wellington 'The Hero of Aliwal' himself died.

He was buried in the town of his birth—Whittlesey.

Sir Harry's popular accolade still adorns the sign of a public house in the town to this day. To be fair to the truth it must be said that Sir Harry was much concerned for his status—perhaps understandably so, since his origins were nowhere near as lofty as many of his peers, at a time when these things very much mattered. It may be, then, that he would not have chosen this as his legacy. Nevertheless, it is something he shares equally with his master—The Iron Duke—together with other great warriors. Perhaps of more relevance—and more importance—in a way peculiar to the British nation, this immortality has ever been the way it has honoured its best loved.

James Humphries

A Short History of the Gwalior War & First Sikh War

Hugh Murray

CHAPTER 1

Gwalior

In the extensive regions between the Sutlej and the Indus, considerable symptoms of disturbance were apparent, and we find official correspondents, early in the following year, giving expression to congratulations that the affairs of British India were in such a tranquil state, as to permit the attention of the governor-general and his council to be devoted to the crisis which seemed to be approaching both in the Punjab and at Gwalior. So early as the month of August, the whole troops in the Agra district received orders to keep themselves in readiness to move at a moment's notice, and it was reported that an army of observation was to be immediately formed, an Army of the Sutlej, under the immediate command of Sir Hugh Gough.

The causes which finally led to a sanguinary revolution in the Punjab, may be thus briefly recapitulated.

Upon the death of Runjeet Sing, in 1839, his favourite wife, after she had ascended the funeral pile, where, along with three others, she was burnt with his corpse, called to her Kurruck Sing, the deceased rajah's son and heir, along with Dhian Sing, his favourite minister, and placing the dead rajah's hand in that of his son, she required the latter to swear to protect and favour his father's minister, and by the like solemn oath bound the minister to be faithful to his new master. Kurruck Sing immediately ascended the throne. He was well-affected to the British government, but possessed none of the talent or energy requisite for so difficult a post. He had not occupied the throne four months when he died, not without strong suspicions of poison, and his son and heir, Now Nehal Sing, who should have succeeded him, was killed by the falling of a beam, as he returned from the funeral pile on which his father's corpse was consumed.

These successive deaths were both ascribed to the intrigues of Runjeet Sing's favourite minister; and, after some difficulty, chiefly arising from the opposition of one of the widows of the latter prince, he succeeded in his long-cherished project of placing Shere Sing on the throne. During the frequent agitations and alarms that ensued, the British government continued to watch their proceedings with some anxiety; but after a time, the affairs of the kingdom, which chiefly owed its formation to the abilities of Runjeet Sing, seemed to acquire some degree of order and settlement, and ceased to attract special attention from the government of India, occupied as it soon was with objects of more pressing interest.

Meanwhile causes of mutual difference and dislike were springing up between the new rajah and his ambitious minister. Various reasons are assigned for these. The Hon. Mr. Osborne, who describes Shere Sing as a fine, manly-looking fellow, adds that he had become especially obnoxious to his minister, in consequence of his attachment to European manners, and his friendly inclinations toward the British, whom Dhian regarded with rancorous hate. This, however, was probably only one of the causes of dissension, sufficing to indicate their disagreement on all questions of general policy. It is stated that the rajah had abandoned himself to the indolent and dissolute habits which have so frequently been the ruin of the native dynasties of India, and that during the frequent dissensions which prevailed between Shere Sing and his powerful minister, the latter went so far as to reproach him in open *durbar* with his dissipation and excesses. Whatever might be the ostensible grounds of dispute, however, the previous character of the minister leaves little room to doubt, that the real ground of offence was the interference with his policy, and the curtailment of his power. He accordingly organized a conspiracy for the assassination of the rajah, in which he enlisted several of the sirdars of the court. His influence with the army is sufficiently apparent, from the time chosen for executing his base design. The rajah had appointed a general review of his troops, at the Dusserah festival, and Ajeet Sing, who is described as an effeminate-looking youth, was selected as the assassin.

The Delhi Gazette thus describes the assassination and the fearful slaughter that followed, in which the faithless originator of it perished, the victim of his own plot:

> Dhian Sing made the arrangement by proposing to the rajah to inspect Ajeet Sing's troops, which he said he would do the following morning, and orders were accordingly issued. On the rajah's arrival on the parade-ground, he found fault with the appearance and condition of some horsemen purposely placed to attract attention, when Ajeet Sing became saucy, words ran high, and, drawing a pistol from his bosom, he shot Shere Sing through the head, the ball having entered his right temple. General Ventura and his party attacked the murderer, but, being opposed by a powerful body of troops, were defeated. Ajeet Sing cut up the rajah's body, placed his head

on a spear, and on entering the town met Prince Purtaub Sing's (Shere's son) *suwarie*, which was immediately attacked, and the prince killed; the palace was taken, and Dhuleep Sing, the only remaining son of Runjeet Sing, a lad ten years old, proclaimed to the throne.

The treasury was thrown open, and the troops paid up their arrears. Troops were sent off to guard all the *ghauts*, and all the opposite party (except Ventura, who escaped) were made prisoners. Ajeet Sing, after having killed Shere Sing, was returning to the fort, and met Dhian; he told him he had done the deed, and asked him to return; he got into Dhian's carriage, and when they got near the gate of the fort, Ajeet Sing stabbed Dhian, and sent his body to his brother and son, Sookhet and Heera Sing. These two individuals surrounded the city with their troops, and the people within continued plundering all night. In the morning, Heera Sing having entered the fort, seized Ajeet Sing, Lena Sing, and others, and having put them to death, exposed their heads in the plain, and threw their bodies into the bazaar. Dhuileep Sing has been put on the *guddee*, and Heera Sing made vizeer.

Six hundred men were slaughtered on both sides.

This barbarous deed was enacted on the 15th September 1843, and by means of it the nominal authority was vested in Dhulleep Sing, a child of ten years old, while that which the unprincipled minister destined for himself, had passed into the hands of Heera Sing, who was now both commander of the army and vizier, and was therefore actual ruler, so long as he could retain the fidelity of the army. Meanwhile the affairs of the court of Gwalior, which occasioned anxiety and distrust, were at length brought to a crisis.

Confusion and anarchy prevailed there, one party deposing another, and successive chiefs struggling for power, while the country was left at the mercy of licentious and undisciplined troops. The British government being bound by its treaties with late rajah to protect his successor, and preserve his territories inviolate, the governor-general could no longer overlook the fact that the conduct of the authorities of Gwalior involved a virtual violation of the treaty. Lord Ellenborough accordingly immediately ordered the advance of troops, sufficient, as he said, "to obtain guarantees for the future security of its own subjects on the common frontier of the two states, to protect the person of the rajah, to quell disturbances within his highness's territories, and to chastise all who shall remain in disobedience."

This was rendered the more imperative by the tender age and helpless position of the rajah, which exposed him to the double danger of being made a tool in the hands of his enemies, and the nominal source of wrongs to his friendly allies. Notwithstanding the preparations which had been made for such an emergency, the commander-in-chief, Sir Hugh Gough, was met by a much stronger and more determined opposition than he had anticipated.

The army had left Agra betwixt the 12th and 18th December, and continued steadily to move on. On the 17th, General Valiant with the advance arrived at Dholpoor. On reaching the *ghaut* opposite Kentree, the Dholpoor Rajah paid a visit of ceremony to the governor-general, and his visit was returned by Lord Ellenborough and the commander-in-chief the following day.

On the 22nd they moved, with the headquarters of the 4th brigade, on Kentree *ghaut*, and the advance, under Sir J. Thackwell, crossed to the right bank of the river. On the 23rd the second division crossed the Chumbul, and proceeded seven miles in the direction of Hingonah, where the advance was encamped. The road was extremely difficult, winding through a steep ravine, scarcely more than twenty feet wide, which a determined enemy might for a time have obstructed almost with impunity. Here for five days the force halted to take rest and counsel.

Bappoo Seetoleah had been despatched from Gwalior negotiations. on the 22nd, and on the following day had an audience with the governor-general, when it was believed in camp that everything was settled the Maharanee and the Sirdars having, it was said, agreed to the terms proposed. On the 24th, the Gwalior Vakeels had a further interview of some duration with the governor-general. Many of the more respectable inhabitants, who came from Gwalior on a visit to the camp, conceived the idea of resistance out of the question. Preparations were made to receive the Maharanee, who was expected in camp on the 28th, with sufficient pomp and circumstance for the rank she held, and audience to which she was about to be admitted.

The governor-general, who had originally been moderate in his demands, requiring the restoration of the Mama Sahib and his friends, the surrender of Khasjee Walla, and dismissal of his partisans,—the exchange of certain portions of country, so as to improve the condition of the mutual frontier—and the disbanding of the mutinous portion of the troops—finally demanding the entire revision of the military establishment, and the surrender of the park of artillery, brought into existence about forty years since by Dowlut Rao Scindia and regarded as the palladium of the state.

This was looked upon as implying the entire destruction of the army, and surrender of the independence of the nation. There is every reason, however, to believe that, throughout, the professions of the Mahratta durbar were hollow and insincere—that so soon as it was found that their earlier and delusive propositions were insufficient to arrest our progress, it was resolved to offer the most determined resistance. Further negotiations appear to have been resorted to merely to gain time. It must always, indeed, form one of the greatest difficulties in the diplomatic intercourse between civilized and semi-barbarous nations, the difficulty of knowing what dependence can be placed on the most solemn asseverations, and professions of good faith.

Among highly civilized nations the value of national credit and unblemished honour is so thoroughly appreciated, that it is rare indeed for the most unprincipled diplomatist to set it at defiance; but among the native princes of India such faithless proceedings as those of the Ameers of Scinde have been too frequent to excite very great surprise. The formidable character and position of the Mahratta army, however, had not been anticipated from the vacillating character of their councils.

The country generally exhibits features offering great natural obstacles to the operations of disciplined forces, being intersected with numerous deep and almost impassable ravines, and gullies, affording great facilities for the irregular tactics of an undisciplined army. It was only by the unceasing labours of the sappers, that a practicable passage was effected for the army under Sir H. Gough; and after passing the Koharee river in three columns, at points considerably distant from each other, the whole British army took up their position by eight o'clock on the morning of the 29th of December 1843, about a mile in front of Maharajpoor.

The Mahrattas had occupied the ground during the previous night, taking up their position with such skill as compelled the commander to alter the disposition of his forces. Seven regiments of Mahratta infantry were ranged in front, each corps having four guns attached to it, which opened on the advanced forces of the British as they took up their ground.

The 39th regiment of British infantry advanced gallantly to the charge, supported by the 66th native infantry. The Mahrattas stood their ground with great bravery, and the British forces sustained a severe loss, their guns doing great execution as they advanced. But no native force has ever been able to withstand the determined charge of the British bayonet. They drove them from their guns into the village, but there the Mahrattas again rallied, and a most sanguinary conflict ensued. After discharging their matchlocks, they flung them from them, and fought hand to hand with the most determined courage.

Meanwhile General Valiant had led on his brigade, and succeeded in taking Maharajpoor in reverse. Twenty-eight guns were captured by this combined movement, but the Mahrattas still stood their ground; nor was their strong position taken till nearly every one of its defenders had been left dead on the spot. The same determined resistance was experienced at every point. They had thrown up entrenchments, and planted their guns with great skill, and in nearly every case the gunners were bayoneted at their posts, without attempting to fly. The consequence was, the loss of the British, both in officers and men, was unusually great. Sir H. Gough, in his despatch to the governor-general, said:

> I regret to say that our loss has been very severe, infinitely beyond what I calculated on; indeed, I did not do justice to the gallantry of my opponents. Their force, however, so greatly exceeded ours, particularly in artillery, the position of their guns was so commanding, they were so well served, and determinedly defended, both by their gunners and their infantry, and the peculiar difficulties of the country giving the defending force so great advantages, that it could not be otherwise.

As usual, where the native forces have displayed peculiar steadiness and skill, it was found that they had had the benefit of more experienced assistance; though they required no aid to give effect to their undisciplined courage and gallant daring. There was found to have been a considerable number of the Company's discharged native infantry, as well as one or two European deserters among the Mahratta troops. One of the latter, it is stated, named Berry, from the 2nd European regiment, had, when he fell, his lighted port-fire in his hand, and fired off his gun, sweeping away fifteen men.

At the same time that the commander-in-chief crossed the Sindean frontiers, Major-General Grey led an auxiliary force towards Punniar, twelve miles south-west of Gwalior, to co-operate with the main body, and place the Mahratta army between two forces, acting in concert. The immense excess of the Mahrattas in point of numbers over the British forces, however, was such as enabled them to counteract this plan of mutual co-operation. A body of 12,000 men, with a large complement of guns, &c. was detached to arrest the progress of Major-General Grey, whose whole force did not amount to a fourth of that number.

The two armies met on the 29th of December, in the vicinity of the fortified village of Mangore, near Punniar, where the Mahrattas had taken up a strong position, and were able to begin the attack at considerable advantage, by assaulting the cumbrous baggage trains which necessarily accompany an Indian army. Towards four o'clock the commander observed the enemy taking up a strong position on a chain of hills to the east of his camp, and resolved on an immediate attack. By a judicious disposition of his forces, the enemy were assailed simultaneously on the centre and left, and completely broken. The whole guns, twenty-four in number, were captured, and all their ammunition, with a portion of treasure, were taken.

The action did not close till nightfall, which prevented the pursuit of the enemy, and enabled them to carry off many of their killed and wounded. Their loss, however, had been very severe, and the occurrence of two such decisive victories on the same day, as those of Maharajpoor and Punniar, effectually put an end to further resistance.

Private accounts would lead to the idea, which the acknowledgments in the despatch of the commander-in-chief may seem in some degree to confirm, that little or no opposition had been anticipated either by the governor-general or the commander-in-chief, both of them probably conceiving that the presence of so large and effective a British force would have sufficed to overawe the rebellious Maharattas.

The commander-in-chief's staff, with the ladies of his family, are said to have been quietly proceeding towards Maharajpoor when the Mahratta guns opened upon them. Lord Ellenborough was likewise present with the ladies of his family; nor was he forced to quit his dangerous and exposed position, until the well-served Mahratta guns gave proof that the elephants of the governor-general, towering over the rear of the 39th regiment, as it took up its position on the field, had become the objects towards which their fire was directed.

The result of the two great battles of Maharajpoor and Punniar destroyed the hopes not only of the mutinous Mahrattas at Gwalior, but of numerous restless mal-contents of Hindustan, and had the effect of diffusing throughout our whole Eastern empire, where the existence of so many races still very partially amalgamated, and curbed in their predatory habits and love of plunder only by the well-directed force of disciplined authority, renders the whole empire peculiarly sensitive to such indirect but powerful influences.

The rajah was installed with great ceremony at Gwalior, in presence of the governor-general, the commander-in-chief, and an immense assemblage of native chiefs. An eyewitness of the imposing ceremonial describes the juvenile rajah as seated beneath a gorgeous canopy of gold, see-sawing his legs beneath his throne according to the fashion of listless schoolboys, seemingly altogether indifferent to the import of the stately proceedings in which he was made to bear so prominent a part.

Meanwhile, however, great and increasing dissatisfaction was expressed in many quarters at the government of Lord Ellenborough. His fondness for military display, and for such pompous exhibitions of vice-regal grandeur as that which immediately followed the victories over the insurgent Mahratta forces, were occasionally government manifested in a way that seemed somewhat inconsistent with the wonted gravity of British rule, and frequently led to the neglect of the civil service and the internal government of India, which were, in fact, his principal duties as governor-general. His whole course of procedure was erratic, and opposed to the definite policy by which the Directory had sought to avert a continued system of aggression on the surrounding native states, and to consolidate the vast possessions over which their rule was only very partially and imperfectly extended.

In the choice of Lord Ellenborough as governor-general, they had calculated on the probable weight of his influence as a civilian, in carrying out measures in accordance with the peaceful line of policy they were anxious to see pursued; but the character of the proceedings of his successor suffice to show that the false glitter of military glory was more seductive to an inexperienced civilian than to a military veteran. A writer, in the Indian Mail of December 1844, remarks of the latter:

> The quiet, unostentatious demeanour of the governor-general has doubtless had its share in tranquilizing India. He has given no intimation, in public at least, of

an intention to quit the Presidency, where he is employed in occupations which befit a man of peace.

In addition, Lord Ellenborough had excited the indignation of the Directorship of the East India Company, by a line of conduct which seemed to imply that he was too well assured of the favour of the Duke of Wellington and the British Cabinet, to greatly concern himself as to the approval his proceedings might meet with from the Directory. Great, therefore, was the sensation created both in India and at home by the sudden recall of Lord Ellenborough, in consequence of the vote of the Court of Directors, in the exercise of their legitimate power, not only without consulting with the government, but in direct opposition to its expressed opinions.

The Duke of Wellington openly and severely censured their proceedings, and it was generally anticipated that an act so embarrassing, if not humiliating, to the government, and to one of its chief leaders, would have led to still more direct collision in the choice of a successor. Such anticipations, however, were not realized. Sir Henry Hardinge was selected to succeed to the important trust. On the 6th of May 1844, he was appointed by the Court of Directors to the office of governor-general of India, and the Crown immediately confirmed the choice. This bold and decisive measure of the Court of Directors excited much discussion and considerable diversity of feeling for a time; but the contrast between the wonted proceedings of Lord Ellenborough, and the unobtrusive course adopted by Lord Hardinge, speedily reconciled all parties interested in the affairs of India to the change of its governor-general.

The country of the Mahrattas still continued in a disorderly and disturbed state, and required the presence of a considerable military force to hold the insurgents in check. Many of the difficulties unquestionably originated in the complicated system of Eastern policy, which has grown out of the circumstances by which a trading company gradually assumed the character of conquerors and rulers. The system of permitting independent or subsidiary princes or rajahs to sway their feeble sceptres within the British dominions has been again and again condemned, as leading to the very worst consequences. British rulers have thereby frequently been unwillingly made accessory to acts of which they could not approve, while such petty principalities become the centres of constant intrigue, and generally prove a barrier to any effectual measures for the improvement of the people.

The Punjab continued for many months to furnish the most novel and unexpected phases of intelligence. Each successive Indian mail brought accounts of new revolutions, massacres, assassinations, and capricious schemings, leading to no definite settlement, and keeping up a feeling of anxiety and alarm throughout our whole Indian possessions, where so many elements exist ready to be excited into opposition and rebellion upon every new impediment or threat of clanger to British supremacy in India.

The army of observation was still maintained on the banks of the Sutlej. From time to time, skirmishes, assaults, and sorties, diversified the dull routine of their passive line of duty, and kept their leaders on the alert. Politicians meanwhile continued to discuss the propriety of the annexation of the Punjab to our Indian empire to round its northern frontiers, and free it from the endless anxiety which must result from the proceedings of a barbarous people in a constant state of revolution, maintaining undisciplined hordes of fierce soldiery ready to take advantage of the first necessity that might induce us to recall the army on their frontier, to make aggressive inroads on our own possessions.

Chapter 2
War in the Punjab

For many months the news of each mail which brought to England information of the state of her vast Eastern possessions, consisted chiefly of confused and alarming rumours of revolutions, tumults, and assassinations, in the state of the Punjab. A large military force was concentrated on the banks of the Sutlej, and war was regarded as inevitable, however long circumstances might delay the commencement of hostilities.

Very great misapprehension however existed, both in India and at home, as to the character of the Sikhs, or the nature of the preparations requisite for meeting any aggressions on their part. So universal was the conviction of their disorderly and mutinous state, and of the want of any supreme power among them, calculated to secure that unanimity of action on which the success of great military movements so greatly depends, that when at length the long-expected collision took place, both the governor-general and the commander-in-chief were found to have overlooked some of the most, indispensable preparations for war. Considering the lengthened period during which war with the Sikhs had been anticipated, and arrangements made for resisting their threatened aggressions, it may well astonish the reader to learn of the difficulties which impeded the first operations of Lord Gough, when hostilities were commenced by the Sikh army crossing the Sutlej.

Captain Cunningham, the impartial historian of the Sikhs, seeks to show that, although the first aggressive movements were undoubtedly made by the Sikhs, the English were guided rather by the selfish and short-sighted policy which guards against immediate danger, than by the wise and honourable foresight which should direct the councils of an enlightened nation when dealing with a people esteemed in every respect their inferiors. He accordingly conceives, that the open preparations for defensive, and, if necessary, for offensive measures, which marked the progress of the army of observation, appeared in the estimation of a rude people as so many acts of designed hostility deliberately marshalled for an attack on their country whenever a convenient opportunity offered. Cunningham says:

> The same defective apprehension which saw no mark of hostility in collecting boats for bridges across a boundary river, and which paid no regard to the effect on a rude people, with more to fear than to hope, of displaying an army with no road before it except that to Lahore, also led the confident English to persevere in despising or misunderstanding the spirit of the disciples of Govind to an extent which almost proved fatal to the continuity of their triumphs. In 1842, the Sikhs were held to be unequal to cope with the Afghans, and even to be inferior in martial qualities to the population of the Jummoo hills. In 1845, the Lahore soldiery was called a 'rabble' in sober official despatches, and although subsequent descriptions allowed the regiments to be composed of the yeomanry of the country, the army was still declared to be daily deteriorating as a military body.

It is, indeed, certain that English officers and Indian Sepoys equally believed they were about to win battles by marching and by the discharge of a few artillery shots, rather than by skilful dispositions, hard fighting, and a prolonged contest. The English not only undervalued their enemy, but they likewise mistook the form which the long-expected aggressions of the Sikhs would assume. It was not thought that the ministry, or even that the army would have the courage to cross the river in force, and to court an equal contest; the known treasonable views of the chiefs, and the unity and depth of feeling which possessed the troops, were equally disregarded, and it continued to be believed that a desultory warfare would sooner or later ensue, which would require the British to interfere, but which would still enable them to do so at their own convenience.

Thus boats for bridges, and regiments and guns, the provocatives to a war, were sufficiently numerous; but food and ammunition, and inefficient carriage and hospital stores, such as were necessary for a campaign, were all behind at Delhi or Agra, or still remained to be collected.

Thus, at the very time when a soldier was at the head of the Indian government, distinguished for military experience as well as for courage and sound judgment, the army was allowed to take the field in every way worse provided and equipped than had been the case when an inexperienced and rash civilian held the office of governor-general.

It is only now that the peculiar characteristics of the Sikhs is coming to be rightly understood. Their origin is traced back to the sixteenth century, when Narruk and Govind, two Khutree prophets, obtained a few converts to a doctrine of religious and social reform, from among the peasants of Lahore and the southern banks of the Sutlej. It is not necessary here, however, to trace their history further than to remark, that by the time the Sikhs came into collision with the British empire in India, they had grown into a powerful nation, bound together not only by social and political ties, but by the still more stringent bonds of a common creed.

The history of Mohammedanism furnishes sufficiently striking evidence of the remarkable effects that may result from such a source, and the Sikhs, or "disciples," appear to be not a whit behind the zeal of the Arabian prophet's followers in their devotion to the Khalsa, or chosen people. The powerful influence of such a bond of union can hardly be overrated, though unfortunately the true character of the Sikh nation was completely misunderstood previous to the war; and the source, as well as the spirit of the continued revolutions which created such alarm on the northern frontiers of British India, entirely escaped the notice of the sagacious diplomatists who conducted our intercourse with that people.

It would now seem, that so far from the revolutions and tumults being the evidences of disunion and revolt among that people, they originated in their devotion to the essential elements of their singular polity, while it was the successive rulers who struggled with them and sought alliances with the English that were in reality mutineers and rebels against the state. Ambition, and the desire for unlimited power, overcame in the minds of successive Sikh rulers the earlier bonds of good faith as members of the Khalsa, but the very cause of alienation between the rulers and the people, supplied a stronger bond of union to the latter.

The soldiery talked of themselves as pre-eminently the Punt'h Khalsajee, or congregation of believers, and their leaders were awed into submission by the resolute spirit with which they were animated. It was by this united and resolute body that successive revolutions were brought about, and one ruler after another dethroned and put to death. Doubtless such a state of things was well calculated to excite uneasiness among neighbouring states, and might perhaps be justly enough characterized both as fanatic and revolutionary, according to more civilized notions of social and political compacts.

Nevertheless, it was manifestly something altogether different from the mutinies and rebellions of an ordinary army of hireling soldiery, such as has most commonly opposed our arms in the East, where the only bond which secures the services of the soldiery is the prospect of pay and plunder. The aspect of the Sikh army, indeed, is one altogether singular, and to a disinterested observer remarkably interesting.

The soldiery are seen animated by a lofty spirit of patriotic daring, aided doubtless by the fierce fire of fanatic zeal, while the Sikh leaders are frequently found secretly counteracting their brave efforts, and more effectually checking their success than the enemy by whom they are openly opposed. As Cunningham says:

> The object of Lal Sing and Tej Sing was not to compromise themselves with the English by destroying an isolated division, but to get their own troops dispersed by the converging forces of their opponents. Their desire was to be upheld as the ministers of a dependent kingdom by grateful conquerors, and they thus deprecated an attack on Ferozepore, and assured the local British authorities of their secret and efficient good will. But these men had also to keep up an appearance of devotion to the interests of their

country, and they urged the necessity of leaving the easy prey of a cantonment untouched, until the leaders of the English should be attacked, and the fame of the Khalsa exalted by the captivity or death of a governor-general.

The Sikh army itself understood the necessity of unity of counsel in the affairs of war, and the power of the regimental and other committees was temporarily suspended by an agreement with the executive heads of the state, which enabled these unworthy men to effect their base objects with comparative ease. Nevertheless, in the ordinary military arrangements of occupying positions and distributing infantry and cavalry, the generals and inferior commanders acted for themselves, and all had to pay come respect to the spirit which animated the private soldiers in their readiness to do battle for the commonwealth of Govind.

The effects of this enthusiastic unity of purpose in an army, headed by men not only ignorant of warfare, but studiously treacherous towards their followers, was conspicuously visible in the speediness with which numerous heavy guns and abundance of grain and ammunition were brought across a large river. Every Sikh considered the cause as his own, and he would work as a labourer as well as carry a musket; he would drag guns, drive bullocks, lead camels, and load and unload boats with a cheerful alacrity, which contrasted strongly with the inapt and sluggish obedience of mere mercenaries, drilled, indeed, and fed with skill and care, but unwarmed by one generous feeling for their country or their foreign employers.

Here, therefore, the Sepoy force, by which so much has been accomplished for British power in India, was opposed by native soldiers, actuated by all the inspiring influences of patriotic feeling, as well as by the wilder fire of fanatic zeal. It was doubly incumbent on British India to lean for safety on the indomitable energy and valour of her European troops, who could alone be safely entrusted to cope with such a foe.

The first acts of aggression were characteristic of the uncivilized race, with whom collision had become inevitable. Intelligence reached Ferozepore, on the 5th of December 1845, that a party of Sikhs had crossed the river and carried off fifty of our camels, with which they had retraced their steps, in order to distribute the booty in their own camp. Several parties of their horse continuing on the left bank, it was deemed advisable, on the same day on which this information arrived, to send off a strong force for the purpose of protecting some military stores that were on their way from Dhurrumkote to Ferozepore.

On the 6th, three days' supplies were ordered to be laid in by the different regiments, and it was supposed that operations against the Sikhs would be commenced without delay. This, however, was not the case, the measure being merely one of precaution. On the 8th, the Sikh troops began to appear in large masses on the right bank of the Sutlej, and their numbers, on the two following days, greatly increased: they had a good deal of artillery with them, which they were constantly discharging.

From opposite Ferozepore, they occupied the bank of the river as far as Hurreekee *ghaut*, some thirty-five miles distance, and considerable parties of their cavalry crossed to the left bank, within their own territory, however, and commenced cutting off supplies, in a manner which led to some apprehensions in Ferozepore that their store of firewood and *bhoosa* might run short. Between the 8th and 11th, thirty more camels were carried off to the other side of the river, making a total of eighty.

On the 9th or 10th, the main body that was opposite Ferozepore changed its position, and moved a little up the river towards the Hurreekee *ghaut*, and a rumour having found its way to Ferozepore on the night of the 10th, that the Sikhs were crossing in numbers, the assistant quartermaster-general, Captain Egerton, was directed to reconnoitre early on the following morning. He went, escorted by a squadron of the 8th light cavalry, and on approaching the point at which he expected to find them, he left the escort behind and rode forward with two orderlies.

The Sikhs were seen to be busy collecting boats about eight miles from Ferozepore, a little beyond our boundary line, and they no sooner perceived Captain Egerton than they fired upon him. It would appear that the men who fired were on the left bank of the river, and only some 600 yards from Captain Egerton. Certain it is that the balls fell around him, and that the moment the firing commenced by the party, the alarm was given in the whole camp, the drums beat to arms, and the whole of the force turned out with great rapidity.

It was now evident to all that a Punjab campaign was inevitable. The whole of the ladies in the governor-general's camp took their departure and returned to Umballah, while orders were issued to troops in all directions to move up with all practicable haste to the frontier. The governor-general paid a hurried visit to Loodiana on the 11th, and inspected the troops there, returning afterwards to Sirhind. The Sikh vakeel at Loodiana received his *conge*, while the British agents at the Lahore court were ordered to withdraw themselves a sure sign of coming hostilities.

By the 12th, about 10,000 Sikhs had crossed the river, with twenty-seven guns, at a place about twelve miles from Ferozepore, and on the 13th they were seven miles from that station, crossing, men and guns, by a bridge of boats, with great activity and expedition. The ladies at Ferozepore were now all sent into the fort for safety, and an immediate attack was expected. On the 13th, the governor-general issued a proclamation, setting forth the views and objects of the British government, and summoning all the chiefs and sirdars of the protected territories to render faithful service against the common enemy.

The Indian mail of February 1846, which brought advices from Bombay up to the 3rd of the previous month, startled all who sympathized in the fortunes of our Eastern empire, with the news that a great battle had been fought on the banks of the Sutlej, while it left the result in the utmost uncertainty. Rumour immensely exaggerated the number of the Sikh forces, and the public mind, still agitated with the recollection of the early reverses in Afghanistan, was thrown anew into a state of feverish excitement by the nature of the information thus imperfectly conveyed.

Sir John Littler had been left with a body of 7,000 men to defend the exposed post of Ferozepore. This was menaced by the overwhelming forces of the Sikhs, but the British commander showed a resolute and undaunted front, and boldly led out his little force to give them battle. Had the Sikh leaders been as resolutely bent on the defeat and extermination of their opponents as the faithful Khalsa were, it may be well doubted if all the heroism of this isolated division of the British army A 7x845 would have saved it from destruction. But Lal Sing and Tej Sing were both probably in greater dread of their Sikh followers than of their British foes, and regarded the chances of victory with greater dread than the prospect of a defeat, which would disperse the enthusiastic Sikhs, who, amid all their fickleness to their leaders, maintained an unimpeachable fidelity to their faith.

A battle, however, had become inevitable, and the rumours which conveyed the first uncertain and contradictory reports, magnified the difficulties experienced by the British forces into renewed disasters, if not absolute defeat. Doubts and fears, however, were speedily dissipated by the arrival of well-authenticated news of victory, though purchased at a cost which served to temper the rejoicings at a partial triumph with many fears.

Chapter 3
Mudki & Ferozeshah

The first battle fought with the Sikhs took place on the 18th of December, between the Ambala and Loodiana divisions of the British army, which had been prudently united by order of Lord Hardinge, and a detachment of the Sikh army under Lal Sing.

The two armies met at Moodkee, twenty miles from Ferozepore, and the Sikhs immediately begun the attack. The whole forces under Lord Gough amounted to about 11,000, while the Sikhs were estimated at 30,000 men, with forty guns. This estimate, however, appears to have greatly exaggerated their number, and Captain Cunningham even inclines to doubt if they much exceeded the British in numbers. The Sikhs were repulsed with severe loss, and seventeen of their guns were taken; but the British learned in the battle of Moodkee the valour of the enemy they had to contend with.

The forces of Lord Gough, already too few, were reduced by a loss of 215 killed and 657 wounded; among the former of whom were Major-Generals Sir Robert Sale and Sir John M'Caskill. The commander-in-chief remarks in his despatch:

> The troops were in a state of great exhaustion, principally from the want of water, which was not procurable on the road, when about three P.M., information

was received that the Sikh army was advancing; and the troops had scarcely time to get under arms, and move to their positions, when the fact was ascertained. I immediately pushed forward the horse artillery and cavalry, directing the infantry, accompanied by the field batteries, to move forward in support.

We had not proceeded beyond two miles when we found the enemy. They evidently had either just taken up this position, or were advancing in order of battle against us. To resist their attack, and to cover the formation of the infantry, I advanced the cavalry under Brigadiers White, Gough, and Mactier, rapidly to the front, in columns of squadrons, and occupied the plain. They were speedily followed by the five troops of horse artillery, under Brigadier Brooks, who took up a forward position, having the cavalry then on his flanks.

The country is a dead flat, covered at short intervals with a low, but, in some places, thick *jhow* jungle, and dotted with sandy hillocks. The enemy screened their infantry and artillery behind this jungle, and such undulations as the ground afforded; and, whilst our twelve battalions formed from echelon of brigade into line, opened a very severe cannonade upon our advancing troops, which was vigorously replied to by the battery of horse artillery under Brigadier Brooke, which was soon joined by the two light field batteries. The rapid and well-directed fire of our artillery appeared soon to paralyse that of the enemy; and, as it was necessary to complete our infantry dispositions without advancing the artillery too near to the jungle, I directed the cavalry under Brigadiers White and Gough to make a flank movement on the enemy's left, with a view of threatening and turning that flank, if possible.

With praiseworthy gallantry, the 3rd light dragoons, with the 2nd brigade of cavalry, consisting of the body guard and 5th light cavalry, with a portion of the 4th lancers, turned the left of the Sikh army, and, sweeping along the whole rear of its infantry and guns, silenced for a time the latter, and put their numerous cavalry to flight. Whilst this movement was taking place on the enemy's left, I directed the remainder of the 4th lancers, the 9th irregular cavalry, under Brigadier Mactier, with a light field battery, to threaten their right. This manoeuvre was also successful. Had not the infantry and guns of the enemy been screened by the jungle, these brilliant charges of the cavalry would have been productive of greater effect.

When the infantry advanced to the attack, Brigadier Brooke rapidly pushed on his horse artillery close to the jungle, and the cannonade was resumed on both sides. The infantry, under Major-Generals Sir Harry Smith, Gilbert, and Sir John M'Caskill, attacked in echelon of lines the enemy's infantry, almost invisible amongst wood and the approaching darkness of night.. The opposition of the enemy was such as might have been expected from troops who had everything at stake, and who had long vaunted of being irresistible. Their ample and extended line, from their great superiority of numbers, far outflanked ours; but this was counteracted by the flank movements of our cavalry. The attack of the infantry now commenced, and the roll of fire from this powerful arm soon convinced the Sikh army that they had met with a foe they little expected. Their whole force was driven from position after position with great slaughter, and the loss of seventeen pieces of artillery, some of them of heavy calibre; our infantry using that never-failing weapon, the bayonet, whenever the enemy stood. Night only saved them from worse disaster, for this stout conflict was maintained during an hour and a half of dim starlight, amidst a cloud of dust from the sandy plain which yet more obscured every object.

The experience acquired by this victory taught the British leaders the necessity for bringing every available means to bear against their brave and resolute enemy. When it became evident that the Sikhs were marching in force towards the Sutlej, bent on assuming the initiative in the war, Lord Hardinge proceeded to the expected scene of contest and made the somewhat novel arrangement of tendering his services as an officer to the commander-in-chief, and assuming the position of second in command under his own subordinate.

By the arrangements which he effected the largest possible force was placed at the command of Lord Gough, to oppose the Sikh invaders. According to the governor-general's despatch, the Sikh army, which occupied the entrenched camp at Ferozeshah, amounted to 60,000 men, while the British forces opposed to them did not exceed 17,000 men. Captain Cunningham, however, in his history, altogether questions the evidence of this very great disparity. He states the forces of the enemy as amounting perhaps to 40,000; but he acknowledges that their numbers were further increased by numerous bodies of undisciplined horse, while their artillery included 150 pieces, served with the most desperate valour, as well as with great coolness and skill:

> At Ferozeshah the larger calibre and greater weight of metal of the mass of the Sikh artillery, and consequently the superiority of practice relatively to that of

the field guns of the English, was markedly apparent in the condition of the two parks after the battle. The captured cannon showed scarcely any marks of round shot or shells, while nearly a third of the British guns were disabled in their carriages or *tumbrils*.

Victory achieved against such a force, by an army composed in part of native mercenaries, and dependent for its sustaining energy and perseverance on the British officers and the European troops, composing a minority of its limited numbers, requires no exaggeration to stamp it with the character of a splendid achievement.

The Sikh army encamped in the form of a horseshoe around the village of Ferozeshah, about ten miles from the scene of their partial defeat at Moodkee, and nearly at an equal distance from Ferozepore. On the 21st of December a junction was effected with Sir John Littler's division, and an immediate attack on the enemy's position was resolved upon; but considerable delay occurred before the arrangements could be completed, and it was within an hour of sunset before the assault was commenced. Captain Cunningham, who fails not in his history to paint the evidences of bravery and military skill displayed by the Sikhs, as well as to expose proceedings of their opponents not likely to be detailed in official gazettes, remarks of the proceedings on the evening of the 21st December:

> The confident English had at last got the field they wanted; they marched in even array, and their famed artillery opened its steady fire. But the guns of the Sikhs were served with rapidity Unexpected and precision, and the foot soldiers stood between and behind the batteries, firm in their order, and active with their muskets. The resistance met was wholly unexpected, and all started with astonishment. Guns were

dismounted, and their ammunition was blown into the air; squadrons were checked in mid career; battalion after battalion was hurled back with shattered ranks, and it was not until after sunset that portions of the enemy's position were finally carried.

Darkness, and confusion of the obstinacy of the contest, threw the English into confusion; men of all regiments and arms were mixed together; generals were doubtful of the fact or of the extent of their own success, and colonels knew not what had become of the regiments they commanded, or of the army of which they formed a part.

Some portions of the enemy's line had not been broken, and the uncaptured guns were turned by the Sikhs upon masses of soldiers oppressed with cold, thirst, and fatigue, and who attracted the attention of the watchful enemy by lighting fires of brushwood to warm their stiffened limbs. The position of the English was one of real danger and great perplexity; their mercenaries had proved themselves good soldiers in foreign countries as well as in India itself, when discipline was little known, or while success was continuous; but in a few hours the five thousand children of a distant land found that their art had been learnt, and that an emergency had arisen which would tax their energies to the utmost.

On that memorable night the English were hardly masters of the ground on which they stood; they had no reserve at hand, while the enemy had fallen back upon a second army, and could renew the fight with increased numbers. The not imprudent thought occurred of retiring upon Ferozepore; but Lord Gough's dauntless spirit counselled otherwise, and his own and Lord Hardinge's personal intrepidity in storming batteries, at the head of troops of English gentlemen and bands of hardy yeomen, eventually achieved a partial success and a temporary repose.

Even the victory of the following day, the candid historian of the Sikhs ascribes fully as much to the faithless pusillanimity of their leaders, as to the skill and valour of the English. The latter were ill provisioned, and suffering from cold and thirst. They were led to the attack on the evening of the 21st, exhausted with fatigue, and unrelieved from hunger and thirst. When night put a temporary close to the action, there was still neither food nor drink to be had, and the exhausted soldiers had to lie down on their arms during that dreadful night, in a state that might well induce the bravest forces. to despond.

Even after they were involved in the fearful struggle of the morrow, they were exposed at one time to the most imminent risk from the failure of the artillery ammunition. With every acknowledgment which candour may induce the generous historian to concede, it cannot be questioned that the indomitable valour of British soldiers was never more strongly displayed than on the bloody field of Ferozeshah.

Whatever amount of their success may have been really due to the infidelity of the Sikh leaders, the whole procedure of the British commanders was entirely independent, if not in ignorance of it. The most credulous, indeed, could attach little value to the co-operation of men who were heading an overwhelming force against which victory had already been twice won with such difficulty and severe losses.

During the battle, both on the 21st and 22nd, the governor-general commanded the left wing of the army, while Lord Gough personally conducted the right. The night that intervened between the commencement and the close of the battle of Ferozeshah must have been one of the deepest anxiety to the British commanders; nor were even the exhausted troops allowed to slumber in peace, where they lay, with their arms at their side, ready with the dawn to renew the bloody struggle. Lord Gough says in his despatch:

> Night fell while the conflict was everywhere raging. Although I now brought up Major-General Sir Harry Smith's division, and he captured and long retained another part of the position, and her Majesty's 3rd light dragoons charged and took some of the most formidable batteries, yet the enemy remained in possession of a considerable portion of the great quadrangle, whilst our troops, intermingled with theirs, kept possession of the remainder, and finally bivouacked upon it, exhausted by their gallant efforts, greatly reduced in numbers, and suffering extremely from thirst, yet animated by an indomitable spirit.
>
> In this state of things the long night wore away. Near the middle of it, one of their heavy guns was advanced, and played with deadly effect upon our troops. Sir Henry Hardinge immediately formed her Majesty's 80th foot and the 1st European light infantry. They were led to the attack by their commanding officers, and animated in their exertions by Lieutenant-Colonel Wood, who was wounded in the outset. The 80th captured the gun, and the enemy, dismayed by this counter-check, did not venture to press on further. During the whole night, however, they continued to harass our troops by fire of service artillery, wherever moonlight discovered our position.
>
> But with daylight came retribution. Our infantry formed in line, supported on both flanks by horse artillery whilst a fire was opened from our centre by such of our heavy guns as remained effective, aided

by a flight of rockets. A masked battery played with great effect upon this point, dismounting our pieces, and blowing up our *tumbrils*. At this moment Lieutenant-General Sir Henry Hardinge placed himself at the head of the left, whilst I rode at the head of the right wing. Our line advanced, and, unchecked by the enemy's fire, drove them rapidly out of the village of Ferozeshah and their encampment; then, changing front to its left, on its centre, our force continued to sweep the camp, bearing down all opposition, and dislodged the enemy from their whole position.

The line then halted, as if on a day of manoeuvre, receiving its two leaders, as they rode along its front, with a gratifying cheer, and displaying the captured standards of the Khalsa army. We had taken upwards of seventy-three pieces of cannon, and were masters of the whole field.

The victory was most opportune, and might well fill the minds of all with joy and gratitude. Nevertheless, though a complete, it was not a decisive victory. The Sikhs had, indeed, been routed and driven from the field. Lord Gough in his despatch says:

> For twenty-four hours not a Sikh has appeared in our front. The remains of the Khalsa army are said to be in full retreat across the Sutlej, or marching up its left bank, towards Hurreekeeputhur, in the greatest confusion and dismay. Their camp is the scene of the most awful carnage, and they have abandoned large stores of grain, camp equipage, and ammunition.

However satisfactory such evidences of flight might be, the narration of the commander- in-chief betrays the fact, that the exhausted victors had been unable to follow in pursuit of the retreating foe, and that the flying Sikhs, who might have been scattered, and irretrievably broken by a timely pursuit, had been allowed to cross the Sutlej at their leisure, and to reform on the opposite bank. The loss of the British was very severe. The official despatches state 694 killed and 1721 wounded, or 2415 in all, amounting to about a seventh of the whole British force in the field.

When the details of the victory of Ferozeshah were reported to the British public through the official despatches, the news was received with gloomy forebodings rather than with the wonted exultations that follow in the train of victory. The commander-in-chief's conduct was made the subject of unsparing criticism. He was blamed alike for his ignorance of the formidable condition of the Sikh army, and for the hardihood with which he had exposed his army to such fearful odds, and incurred the risk of defeat as well as the certainty of such severe loss as his despatches acknowledged.

Even his tactics in the field were freely discussed and censured, and the excited critics seemed disposed to make the British general responsible alike for the bravery of the Sikhs, and for his own inferiority in numbers and artillery. The want of proper supplies both of provisions and ammunition was unquestionably an oversight of the gravest nature, though not justly chargeable on the commander-in-chief. From the want of the latter, the British forces were compelled to remain inactive while the Sikhs re-crossed the Sutlej in great force, and proceeded to construct a bridge head by which to secure the passage of the river. The commander- in-chief feared to oppose these proceedings of his beaten foe, lest an attack on his part should bring on another general engagement, while they were so deficient in ammunition that their artillery must have been nearly useless, and they were even prevented from attacking some petty forts which still overawed the neighbouring population, and checked the march of convoys and detachments whose approach was so indispensable to them.

The battle of Ferozeshah threatened to prove a fruitless victory. By the capture of Dhurmkot, the safe transit of grain to the army was rendered more secure; but the march of the large convoy of guns, ammunition, and treasure, for want of which the British forces had been compelled to remain inactive, was not accomplished without a severe skirmish, in which 137 were killed or wounded, and, what was felt still more, several of the British were left prisoners in the hands of the Sikhs. Captain Cunningham says:

> Every beast of burden, which had not got within sight of Loodiana, or which had not, timorously but prudently, been taken back to Jugraon, when the firing was heard, fell into the hands of the Sikhs, and they were enabled boastfully to exhibit artillery store carts as if they had captured British cannon.
>
> Loodiana was relieved; but an unsuccessful skirmish added to the belief, so pleasing to the prostrate princes of India, that the dreaded army of their foreign masters had at last been foiled by the skill and valour of the disciples of Govind, the kindred children of their own soil.
>
> The British sepoys glanced furtively at one another, or looked towards the east, their home; and the brows of Englishmen themselves grew darker as they thought of struggles rather than triumphs. The governor-general and commander-in-chief trembled for the safety of that siege train and convoy of ammunition, so necessary to the efficiency of an army which they had launched in haste against aggressors, and received back shattered by the shock of opposing arms.

Sir Harry Smith, the leader of the beaten brigades, saw before him a tarnished name after the labours of a life, nor was he met by many encouraging hopes of rapid retribution. The Sikhs on their side were correspondingly elated; the presence of European prisoners added to their triumph.

The Sikhs seemed about to retrieve their losses, and march victorious into the British dominions. Golab Sing was chosen their leader, and with the unanimity and vigour of determined councils and a definite plan of action, the Khalsa forgot their previous losses and boasted that the British army should be annihilated, or driven in dishonour from the field. But the time was gone when unity in the councils of Sikhs could secure their triumph over the conquerors of the East.

Chapter 4
Aliwal

Sir Harry Smith was the first to give the check to those who had momentarily tarnished his well-won reputation. With the reinforcements he had received, which raises the forces under his command to 11,000 men, he marched on the 28th of January 1846, determined to give the enemy battle. The commander-in-chief had reinforced him on the 26th both with cavalry and guns, and on the following day he occupied their deserted position.

The Sikhs retreated about ten miles, towards the banks of the Sutlej, where they were joined by a reinforcement, which raised their forces to fully 15,000 men, and they took up a position, with the village of Aleewal on their left, and threw up banks of earth to protect their line in front, and oppose additional impediments to their assailants. Sir Harry Smith's narrative of the battle which followed is characterised by singular coolness and precision:

> As I neared the enemy the ground became most favourable for the troops to manoeuvre, being open and hard grass land. I ordered the cavalry to take ground to the right and left by brigades, thus displaying the heads of the infantry columns, and as they reached the hard ground I directed them to deploy into line. Brigadier Godby's brigade was in direct echelon to the rear of

the right, the Shekawatte Infantry in like manner to the rear of my left. The cavalry in direct echelon on, and well to the rear of both flanks of the infantry. The artillery massed on the right, and centre and left.

After deployment I observed the enemy's left to outflank me, I therefore broke into open columns and took ground to my right: when I had gained sufficient ground, the troops wheeled into line; there was no dust, the sun shone brightly. The manoeuvres were performed with the celerity and precision of the most correct field-day. The glistening of the bayonets and swords of this order of battle was most imposing, and the line advanced.

Scarcely had it moved forward 150 yards, when, at ten o'clock, the enemy opened a fierce cannonade from his whole line. At first his balls fell short, but quickly reached us. Thus upon him, and capable of better ascertaining his position, I was compelled to halt the line, though under fire, for a few moments, until I ascertained that by bringing up my right and carrying the village of Aleewal, I could with great effect precipitate myself upon his left and centre.

The capture of the village proved an easier task than was anticipated. The holders of the post speedily gave way before the determined charge of the British brigades. The Sikhs stood their ground on the field, however, with the most resolute valour, and even threatened at one time to out-flank the right wing of the British. Sir Harry Smith says:

> The enemy fought with much resolution; they maintained frequent reencounters with our cavalry hand to hand. In one charge of infantry upon Her Majesty's 16th lancers, they threw away their muskets, and came on with their swords and targets against the lance.

But their brave resistance proved unavailing. They made several ineffectual attempts to rally but at length were driven across the Sutlej, with immense loss, and in the utmost confusion and terror. The whole artillery of the enemy was either captured or destroyed, 52 guns remained in the hands of the victors. The whole of the Sikh camp, baggage, stores of ammunition, grain, and nearly everything brought into the field remained as the spoils of the conquerors, and the commander exultingly exclaims in his despatch:

> I am unwont to praise when praise is not merited, and I here must avowedly express my firm opinion and conviction that no troops in any battle on record ever behaved more nobly.

The victory of Aleewal was one of the most important that has ever been gained by the British forces in India. The number engaged was indeed comparatively small. But the effect of this opportune defeat of the Sikhs, at the very time when they were rejoicing in united councils and exulting in anticipated victory, completely overthrew their whole schemes. Golab Sing instead of attempting to rally his defeated forces upbraided them with the rashness and folly of hoping to overcome the conquerors of India, and immediately opened negotiations with the English commander.

Another battle, however, had to be fought, and another victory won, before the conquerors could dictate terms to the hardy and resolute race whom they encountered on the northern boundaries of British empire in the East. The terms offered by the British leaders in reply to the negotiations were such as must be acknowledged to afford reasonable evidence of the integrity of their motives, in entering on the contest. They disclaimed all desire of annexation or conquest, and intimated their readiness to acknowledge a Sikh sovereignty in Lahore, so soon as the army should be disbanded. But, however reasonable and even generous such terms might appear to those that dictated them, they struck at the very root of the Khalsa's dreams of supremacy and integrity, and if the historian of the Sikhs is to be relied upon, the battle of singular Sobraon, which followed these abortive negotiations, was fought with a perfect understanding with the faithless rajah, that in case of British arms being once more victorious, the Sikh army should be openly abandoned by its own government, and that the victors should pass the Sutlej unchecked, and march without opposition to the capital.

The conditional terms of a negotiation thus mutually agreed upon by belligerent leaders, preparatory to once more appealing to the arbitration of battle, are probably unparalleled in the history of ancient or modern warfare. They suffice, however, to show the singular footing on which our vast Eastern empire rests, and how difficult it is to judge of the proceedings of those to whom its conduct is committed, or by whom its progress is opposed, according to any standard of European policy.

The Sikhs, meanwhile, were not wanting in preparation for renewing the contest. The brilliant achievement of Sir Harry Smith's division at Aleewal, had been conducted with an amount of boldness, caution, and military skill, worthy of a brave and experienced commander, and it had been productive of the happiest effects on British interests in India, nevertheless it was only the victory of a division. Its moral effect in confirming the courage and high faith in the destiny of British arms of the one party, and in moving the opposite party to despondency and dread, was doubtless great.

Fortune had deserted the Khalsa. Defeat and subjection already depended over them, and divided councils were hurrying on their fate. A decisive victory was, however, still needed, ere the British could force the passage of the Sutlej, and become masters of the Punjab. Prompt measures were indispensably required.

To subjugate the Punjab in one season, by force of arms, was a task of difficult achievement and full of imminent risks. The dominion of the English in India hinges mainly upon the number and efficiency of the troops of their own race which they can bring into the field. But besides this, it was felt that the minds of men throughout India were agitated, and that protracted hostilities would not only jeopardize the communications with the Jumna, but might disturb the whole of the north-western provinces, swarming with a military population which is ready to follow any standard affording pay or allowing plunder, and which already sighs for the end of a dull reign of peace.

Bright visions of standing triumphant on the Indus and of numbering the remotest conquests of Alexander among the provinces of Britain, doubtless warmed the imagination of the governor- general; but the first object was to drive the Sikhs across the Sutlej by force of arms, or to have them withdrawn to their own side of the river by the unconditional submission of the chiefs and the delegates of the army; for, until that were done, no progress could be said to have been made in the war, and every petty chief in Hindustan would have silently prepared for asserting his independence, or for enlarging his territory on the first opportunity.

This critical state of things in our Indian empire has long been felt by the few earnest thinkers, on whom the false glare of military glory exercises no blinding influence. Even the short-sighted policy of self-interested motives has sufficed to awaken the Home Directory to a sense of it; and for many years each successive governor has been warned against any further aggressive movements, or the annexation of additional domains to the already unwieldy empire which owns our sway.

It is easier, however, to dictate a theory of policy, than to control the events by which it must ultimately be modified. Some of the later wars have perhaps been justly characterized as aggressive, notwithstanding the necessity which frequently compelled the first movements which were thought to render the rest indispensable to the safety of our former possessions, but others of them were reluctantly begun, and only boldly and effectively carried on as the safest and swiftest means of preventing their recurrence.

While Sir Harry Smith was manoeuvring his division, the indispensable reinforcements were being brought up from the rear, the main body of the Sikhs had been no less active in their preparations for the final struggle. They had gradually brought the greater part of their available force into an entrenched camp formed on the left bank of the Sutlej, and which comprised within its irregular ramparts the whole possessions they still held by force of arms in the British dominions. Their force was estimated at 35,000 fighting men, though Captain Cunningham inclines to think that such an estimate greatly exceeds the truth. He adds, moreover, that their works exhibited marked evidence of a want of unity of design, the soldiers doing everything and the leaders nothing.

It is probable, however, that in this the candid historian of the Sikhs ascribes to want of unity of purpose what should rather be ascribed only to imperfect knowledge and inferior skill. It was hardly to be expected that an experienced military engineer, as he is known to be, should find in the Sikh entrenchments a satisfactory display of engineering skill, even although there were European officers of acknowledged experience and great bravery in command of some of their divisions. But the defeat at Aleewal, which had proved so welcome and so important in its results to the British, had a corresponding depressive effect on the Sikhs.

Some of the older and more experienced Sikh chiefs looked forward with sad forebodings to the approaching contest, and one favourite leader, Sham Sing, announced to the desponding Khalsa his resolution to meet death in the foremost ranks that engaged with the enemy, and so to offer himself up as a sacrifice on behalf of the sacred commonwealth, threatened with such impending danger.

Confidence and joyful anticipations of triumph prevailed throughout the British camp. The victory of Aleewal had restored the faith of the Sepoys in the fortune of British arms, while the European forces exulted in the anticipation of victory. Substantial grounds of confidence had meanwhile been supplied by the arrival of the heavy ordnance, with abundant ammunition and stores. The obstacles which had impeded their earlier operations, and made victory so difficult and so hardly won, no longer existed to check the bold advance of the British forces, or the daring impetuosity of the commander- in-chief.

Chapter 5

Sobraon

The 10th of February, only twelve days after the victory of Aleewal, was fixed for storming the Sikh position, and driving them beyond the river. Through indifference or neglect, the British had allowed a post of observation of some importance to fall into the hands of the Sikhs, and the surprising of this was determined upon as the first proceeding.

Long before dawn, the whole British camp was in motion, and an advanced position. party was ordered to drive in the enemy's pickets. The additional gloom of a thick haze added to the darkness of the night, as the British forces silently advanced to assume the initiative in the contest, but the posts of observation, both at the Sobraon and in front of Koodeewalla, were found unoccupied, though held by a strong force on the previous day. The Sikhs were everywhere taken by surprise, and beat loudly to arms throughout their wide entrenchments on both sides of the river. The English heavy ordnance had been arranged in masses on some of the most commanding points opposite the enemy's entrenchments, and at sunrise the batteries opened upon them.

For three hours the deadly shower of iron hail poured down upon the Sikh forces within their entrenchments, mingled with the more deadly shells, that scattered death on every side as they fell. But the Sikh entrenchments bristled with the heavy ordnance which had told so effectively against the light fieldpieces that formed the sole British artillery in the earlier engagements, and the sun's level rays hardly pierced through the clouds of sulphurous smoke that loomed over the scene of deadly strife. The commander-in-chief says in his despatch:

> Our battery of nine-pounders opened near the little Sobraon, with a brigade of howitzers formed from the light field batteries and troops of horse artillery, shortly after daybreak. But it was half-past six before the whole of our artillery fire was developed. It was most spirited and well directed; but notwithstanding the formidable calibre of our iron guns, mortars, and howitzers, and the admirable way in which they were served, and aided by a rocket battery, it would have been visionary to expect that they could, within any limited time, silence the fire of seventy pieces behind well constructed batteries of earth, plank, and fascines, or dislodge troops covered either by redoubts or epaulements, or within a treble line of trenches.
>
> The effect of the cannonade was, as has since been proved by an inspection of the camp, most severely felt by the enemy; but it soon became evident that the issue of this struggle must be brought to the arbitrament of musketry and the charge of bayonet.
>
> At nine o'clock, Brigadier Stacey's brigade, supported on either flank by Captains Horsford's and Fordyce's batteries, and Lieutenant-Colonel Lane's troop of horse artillery, moved to the attack in admirable order. The infantry and guns aided each other correlatively.

The former marched steadily on in line, which they halted only to correct when necessary. The latter took up successive positions at the gallop, until at length they were within three hundred yards of the heavy batteries of the Sikhs; but, notwithstanding the regularity, and coolness, and scientific character of this assault, which Brigadier Wilkinson well supported, so hot was the fire of cannon, musketry, and *zumboorucks*, kept up by the Khalsa troops, that it seemed for some moments impossible that the entrenchments could be won under it; but soon persevering gallantry triumphed, and the whole army had the satisfaction to see the gallant Brigadier Stacey's soldiers driving the Sikhs in confusion before them within the area of their encampments.

The resistance of the Sikhs was terrible. The deadly fire of their muskets and well-served artillery, mowed down the advancing lines of the British, and compelled them to give way. The first assailants were repulsed, but they rallied and returned to the charge, and, supported by the advance of the second division, after a severe struggle, they obtained possession of some of the enemy's most important batteries in the front. Still the Sikhs stood their ground. No panic seized these hardy enthusiasts, though thus assailed within their own entrenchments.

One point after another was forced. The sappers levelled spaces sufficient for the cavalry to pour into their camp, and sustain the efforts of the infantry who had borne the brunt of the deadly struggle. But still the Sikhs fought with all the wild fury of despair. Single batteries still held out, and hundreds fell in the attempt to arrest their persevering efforts to retrieve the hopeless fortunes of the Khalsa. Captain Cunningham says:

The interior was filled with courageous men, who took advantage of every obstacle, and fought fiercely for every spot of ground. The traitor, Tej Sing, indeed, instead of leading fresh men to sustain the failing strength of the troops on his right, fled on the first assault, and, either accidentally or by design, sank a boat in the middle of the bridge of communication.

But the ancient Sham Sing remembered his vow; he clothed himself in simple white attire, as one devoted to death, and calling on all around him to fight for the Guru, who had promised everlasting bliss to the brave, he repeatedly rallied his shattered ranks, and at last fell a martyr on a heap of his slain countrymen. Others might be seen standing on the ramparts amid showers of balls, waving defiance with their swords, or telling the gunners where the fair-haired English pressed thickest together.

Along the stronger half of the battlements, and for a period of half an hour, the conflict raged sublime in all its terrors. The parapets were sprinkled with blood from end to end; the trenches were filled with the dead and the dying.

Amid the deafening roar of cannon, and the multitudinous fire of musketry, the shouts of triumph or of scorn were yet heard, and the flashing of innumerable swords was yet visible; or from time to time exploding magazines of powder, threw bursting shells, beams of wood and banks of earth, high above the agitated sea of smoke and flame which enveloped the host of combatants, and for a moment arrested the attention amid all the din and tumult of the tremendous conflict. But gradually each defensible position was captured, and the enemy was pressed towards the scarcely fordable river.

Yet, although assailed on either side by squadrons of horse and battalions of foot, no Sikh offered to submit, and no disciple of Govind asked for quarter. They everywhere showed a front to the victors, and stalked slowly and sullenly away, while many rushed singly forth to meet assured death by contending with a multitude. The victors looked with stolid wonderment upon the indomitable courage of the vanquished, and forbore to strike when the helpless and the dying frowned unavailing hatred.

But the warlike rage, or the calculating policy of the leaders, had yet to be satisfied, and, standing with the slain heaped on all sides around them, they urged troops of artillery almost into the waters of the Sutlej to more thoroughly destroy the army which had so long scorned their power.

No deity of heroic fable received the living within the oozy gulfs of the oppressed stream, and its current was choked with added numbers of the dead, and crimsoned with the blood of a fugitive multitude. But vengeance was complete; the troops, defiled with dust and smoke and carnage, stood mute indeed for a moment, until the glory of their success rushing upon their minds, they gave expression to their feelings, and hailed their victorious commanders with reiterated shouts of triumph and congratulation.

Never before had British arms been opposed to such determined bravery and skill, as strove with them on that bloody plain. The deadly struggles which had hung disgrace for a time on the British banners in the passes of Afghanistan, owed their fatal terrors to the natural character of the country, far more than to the bravery of its hardy but undisciplined forces. But here they were withstood on a fair field by a foe that listened unappalled to the thunders of their cannon, and stood unmoved before the glittering points of their bayonets when laid to the charge. Even the brave Sikhs. however, sustained by all the nerve that fanaticism can add to native valour, found British skill and daring more, than a match for them on an equal field. The British commander says, in his despatch from the field of battle:

> At one time the thunder of full 120 pieces of ordnance reverberated in this mighty combat through the valley of the Sutlej; and as it was soon seen that the weight of the whole force within the Sikh camp was likely to be thrown upon the two brigades that had passed its trenches, it became necessary to convert into close and serious attacks the demonstrations with skirmishers and artillery of the centre and right; and the battle raged with inconceivable fury from right to left.
>
> The Sikhs, even when at particular points their entrenchments were mastered with the bayonet, strove to regain them by the fiercest conflict sword in hand. Nor was it until the cavalry of the left, under Major-general Sir Joseph Thackwell, had moved forward, and ridden through the openings of the entrenchments made by our sappers, in single file, and reformed as they passed them, and the 3rd dragoons, whom no obstacle usually held formidable by horse appears to check, had on this day, as at Ferozeshah, galloped over and cut down the obstinate defenders of batteries and field-works, and until the full weight of three divisions of infantry, with every field artillery gun which could be sent to their aid, had been cast into the scale, that victory finally declared for the British.
>
> The fire of the Sikhs first slackened, and then

nearly ceased, and the victors then pressing them on every side, precipitated them in masses over the bridge, and into the Sutlej, which a sudden rise had rendered hardly fordable. In their efforts to reach the right bank, through the deepened water, they suffered from our horse artillery a terrible carnage. Hundreds fell under this cannonade; hundreds upon hundreds were drowned in attempting the perilous passage.

Their awful slaughter, confusion, and dismay, were such as would have excited compassion in the hearts of their generous conquerors, if the Khalsa troops had not, in the early part of the action, sullied their gallantry by slaughtering and barbarously mangling every wounded soldier whom, in the vicissitudes of attack, the fortune of war left at their mercy. 67 pieces of cannon, upwards of 200 camel Trophies of swivels (*zumboorucks*), numerous standards, and vast munitions of war, captured by our troops, are the pledges and trophies of our victory. The battle was over by eleven in the morning, and in the forenoon I caused our engineers to burn a part and to sink a part of the vaunted bridge of the Khalsa army, across which they had boastfully come once more to defy us, and to threaten India with ruin and devastation.

The victory was complete; but it was not purchased without a severe loss on the part of the victors; 320 British soldiers lay dead on the field, including Major-General Sir Robert Dick, a veteran soldier, who had served with honour in the Peninsula and at Waterloo; Brigadier Taylor, and other distinguished officers, who fell while leading on their men, or recalling them to a sense of their duty, as they recoiled from the deadly fire of the enemy. In addition to these, the British had 2,083 wounded, some of them fatally.

But the loss of the Sikhs did not amount to less than 8,000, while they were irretrievably broken and scattered, without hope of again being able to take the field. The commander-in-chief says:

> We have to deplore a severe loss, but certainly not heavy when weighed in the balance against the obstacles overcome and the advantages gained.

That same the night several regiments were pushed across the Sutlej opposite Ferozepore, but no enemy appeared to resist their progress. On the 11th the British forces pushed on to Kussoor, and on the following day its fortress was occupied by them without opposition. On the 13th the British army encamped under the walls of that ancient town. They learned there that the Sikhs had reassembled to the amount of 20,000 men; but they were no longer formidable to the victorious invaders of the Punjab. Their whole artillery and munitions of war were in the hands of the enemy. The power of the Khalsa was effectually broken, and no force of innate courage or fanatic zeal could replace to it the indefensible provisions for continuing the struggle, or even restoring the confidence which had before nerved them to the fight, and upheld them with the hope of victory even after repeated defeats.

CHAPTER 6

Peace

The official proclamation of the governor-general, issued only four days after the victory of Sobraon, contains both a declaration and a defence of British policy. It thus proceeds to announce, and to justify the course pursued under the immediate surveillance of the governor-general, who had combined in so unwonted a man the duties of the civilian and the soldier.

The British army has crossed the Sutlej, and entered the Punjab. The governor-general announces by this proclamation that that measure has been adopted by the government of India, in accordance with the intentions expressed in the proclamation of the 13th of December last, as having been forced upon the governor-general for the purpose of 'effectually protecting the British provinces, for vindicating the authority of the British government, and for punishing the violators of treaties and the disturbers of the public peace.'

These operations will be steadily persevered in and vigorously prosecuted, until the objects proposed to be accomplished are fully attained. The occupation of the Punjab by the British forces will not be relinquished until ample atonement for the insult offered to the British government by the infraction of the treaty of 1809, and by the unprovoked invasion of the British provinces, shall have been exacted. These objects will include full indemnity for all expenses incurred during the war, and such arrangements for the future government of the Lahore territories as will give perfect security to the British government against similar acts of perfidy and aggression.

Military operations against the government and army of the Lahore state have not been undertaken by the government of India from any desire of territorial aggrandizement. The governor-general, as already announced in the proclamation of the 13th of December, 'sincerely desired to see a strong Sikh government re-established in the Punjab, able to control its army, and to protect its subjects.' The sincerity of these professions is proved by the fact, that no preparations for hostilities had been made when the Lahore government suddenly, and without a pretext of complaint, invaded the British territories.

The unprovoked aggression has compelled the British government to have recourse to arms, and to organize the means of offensive warfare, and whatever may now befall the Lahore state, the consequences can alone be attributed to the misconduct of that government and its army. No extension of territory was desired by the government of India; the measures necessary for providing indemnity for the past and security for the future will, however, involve the retention by the British government of a portion of the country hitherto under the government of the Lahore state. The extent of territory which it may be deemed advisable to hold will be determined by the conduct of the durbar, and by considerations for the security of the British frontier. The government of India will, under any circumstances, annex to the British provinces the districts, hill and plain, situated between the rivers Sutlej and Beeas, the revenues thereof being appropriated as a part of the indemnity required from the Lahore state.

From the sketch we have already drawn of the singular religious commonwealth of the Sikhs, the reader will readily perceive that, however consistent with sound policy and the just claims of the victors the proposed terms might appear, they were dictated without any reference to the peculiar consistency of the Sikh commonwealth, if not indeed in ignorance of the peculiar features on which it was based.

For the British governor-general to dictate terms by which a government might be established in the Punjab capable of controlling the Sikh army, might not unreasonably be compared to the liberal offers of the English Edward to Baliol, on condition that he should control the patriot army of Scotland. The defence of British policy, however, lies in the fact that, whoever may be justly chargeable with the initiative in the war, the movements of the British was purely defensive. They desired no accession of territory, and did not seek to interfere in the control of the Sikh soldiers, until their revolutionary movements menaced the British frontier, and endangered the peace and safety of the empire.

In the conclusion of the same official proclamation, the governor-general thus confidently appeals to the integrity of purpose which had influenced the whole course of British policy.

> The governor-general, at this moment of a most complete and decisive victory, cannot give a stronger proof of the forbearance and moderation of the British government than by making this declaration of his

intentions, the terms and mode of the arrangement remaining for further adjustment. The governor-general, therefore, calls upon all those chiefs who are the well-wishers of the descendants of Runjeet Sing, and especially such chiefs as have not participated in the hostile proceedings against the British power, to act in concert with him in carrying into effect such arrangements as shall maintain a Sikh government at Lahore, capable of controlling its army and protecting its subjects, and based upon principles that shall provide for the future tranquillity of the Sikh states, shall secure the British frontier against a repetition of acts of aggression, and shall prove to the whole the moderation and justice of the paramount power of India.

If this opportunity of rescuing the Sikh nation from military anarchy and misrule be neglected, and hostile opposition to the British h army be renewed, the government of India will make such other arrangements for the future government of the Punjab as the interests and security of the British power may render just and expedient.

If the Sikh soldiers did not acquiesce in the justice of British policy, which dictated the necessity for a supreme and independent power by which their future motions would be controlled and kept in check, they at least acknowledged the right of dictation which victory had placed in the conquerors of Sobraon. They agreed to authorize their chosen minister, Golab Sing, to treat with the British, and empowered him to concur in arrangements on the basis announced in the proclamation, of recognizing a Sikh government in Lahore.

On the 15th of February, the governor-general was visited at Kussoor by the rajah and several of the most influential Sikh chiefs, to whom he stated the terms upon which he was willing to conclude a peace. These included the recognition of Dhuleep Sing as sovereign of Lahore, but required the cession of the country between the Beeas and the Sutlej, as specified in the proclamation. They were likewise required to pay to the conquerors a million and a half sterling, as some indemnity for the expenses of the war. The governor-general was induced to dictate humiliating terms, in order that the conviction of the supremacy and invincibility of British arms might be felt wherever rebellious thoughts had been cherished, among the allies or the dependents of our Indian empire.

After vain endeavours to evade some of the most unpalatable requirements, the Sikh chiefs reluctantly accepted the offered terms, and the young rajah personally tendered his submission. Still more effectually to demonstrate how effectually the Khalsa was humbled under the supremacy of their conquerors, the British army entered Lahore on the 20th February, and, two days afterwards, an English garrison occupied the citadel of the Sikh capital.

In the arrangements which followed, Golab Sing contrived that his own interests should be advanced, however those of the great body of the disciples of Govind might suffer. His influence with the Sikh forces, and his own wealth both in treasure and munitions of war, rendered him still formidable, should he be driven, by the exacting demands of his conquerors, to fall back on the support of the Sikhs. Captain Cunningham thus narrates this part of the transactions in the Punjab:

> The low state of the Lahore treasury, and the anxiety of Lal Sing to get a dreaded rival out of the way, enabled the governor-general to appease Golab Sing in a manner sufficiently agreeable to the rajah

himself, and which still further reduced the importance of the successor of Runjeet Sing. The rajah of Jummoo did not care to be simply the master of his native mountains; but as two-thirds of the pecuniary indemnity required from Lahore could not be made good, territory was taken instead of money, and Cashmere and the hill states from the Beeas to the Indus were cut off from the Punjab proper, and transferred to Golab Sing, as a separate sovereign, for a million pounds sterling.

The arrangement was a dexterous one, if reference be only had to the policy of reducing the power of the Sikhs; but the transaction scarcely seems worthy of the British name and greatness, and the objections become stronger when it is considered that Golab Sing had agreed to pay sixty-eight *lacs* of rupees—£680,000—as a fine to his paramount, before the war broke out, and that the custom of the East as well as of the West requires the feudatory to aid his lord in foreign war and domestic strife. Golab Sing ought thus to have paid the deficient million of money as a Lahore subject, instead of being put in possession of Lahore provinces as an independent prince.

The succession of the rajah was displeasing to the Sikhs generally, and his separation was the less in accordance with his own aspirations than the ministry of Runjeet Sing's empire; but his rise to sovereign power excited nevertheless the ambition of others, and Tej Sing, who knew his own wealth, and was fully persuaded of the potency of gold, offered twenty-five *lacs* of rupees for a princely crown and another dismembered province. He was chid for his presumptuous misinterpretation of English principles of action; the arrangement with Golab Sing was the only one of the kind which took place, and the new ally was formally invested with the title of Maharajah at Amritsar, on the 15th March 1846. But a portion of the territory at first proposed to be made over to him was reserved by his masters, the payments required from him were reduced by a fourth, and they were rendered still more easy of liquidation by considering him to be the heir to the money which his brother Soochet Sing had buried in Ferozepore.

Captain Cunningham then describes this influential Sikh chief, in a note which he appends to the previous narrative:

> In the course of this history there has, more than once, been occasion to allude to the unscrupulous character of Rajah Golab Sing; but it must not therefore be supposed that he is a man malevolently evil. He will, indeed, deceive an enemy and take his life without hesitation, and in the accumulation of money he will exercise many oppressions; but he must be judged with reference to the morality of his age and race, and to the necessities of his own position. If these allowances be made, Golab Sing will be found an able and moderate man, who does little in an idle or wanton spirit, and who is not without some traits both of good humour and generosity of temper.

The spirit of the Sikh soldiery, however, was not broken by their reverses, though they had doubtless learned to acknowledge the superiority of British arms. But for such a formidable power to check this enthusiastic soldiery of the creed of Govind, it is difficult to conceive what might ultimately have proved the limits of their conquests. Captain Cunningham thus describes their deportment in the presence of their conquerors:

While the governor-general and commander-in-chief remained at Lahore at the head of 20,000 men, portions of the Sikh army came to the capital to be paid up and disbanded. The soldiers showed neither the despondency of mutinous rebels nor the effrontery and indifference of mercenaries, and their manly deportment added lustre to that valour which the victors had dearly felt and generously extolled.

The men talked of their defeat as the chance of war, or they would say that they were mere imitators of unapproachable masters. But amid all their humiliation, they inwardly dwelt upon their future destiny with unabated confidence; and while gaily calling themselves inapt and youthful scholars, they would sometimes add, with a significant and sardonic smile, that the Khalsa itself was yet a child, and that as the commonwealth of Sikhs grew in stature, Govind would clothe his disciples with irresistible might and guide them with unequalled skill. Thus brave men sought consolation, and the spirit of progress which collectively animated them yielded with a murmur to the superior genius of England and civilization, to be chastened by the rough hand of power, and perhaps to be moulded to noblest purposes by the informing touch of knowledge and philosophy.

Such is the account furnished by the pen of a generous British soldier, of the hardy insurgents who assailed the north western frontier of British India, and were thus hardly defeated, after repeated battles under the most undaunted of British generals.

British arms were again triumphant. New additions were, temporarily or permanently, annexed to our Indian empire, forced on us by circumstances or necessity. New duties and cares helped to complicate the difficulties of our Indian policy, while sanguine politicians flattered themselves that the long sought natural boundaries of Hindustan had at length been reached, and that the British soldier might now sheath his sword, unless as the weapon of defensive justice against aggression.

What the final results of the first campaign in the Punjab may yet prove to be, it is vain for the historian to speculate; but the view we have endeavoured to give of the singular race of armed zealots who constitute the Sikh commonwealth, is alone sufficient to satisfy the reader that it would be folly to anticipate the reverses of a single campaign could suffice to reduce them to contented subjects, or peaceable and trustworthy allies. A much briefer experience than the least hopeful could have anticipated, served to show on how uncertain a tenure peace could be established with them.

ALSO FROM LEONAUR
AVAILABLE IN SOFTCOVER OR HARDCOVER WITH DUST JACKET

THE COMPLEAT RIFLEMAN HARRIS by Benjamin Harris as told to & transcribed by Captain Henry Curling—The adventures of a soldier of the 95th (Rifles) during the Peninsular Campaign of the Napoleonic Wars

WITH WELLINGTON'S LIGHT CAVALRY by William Tomkinson—The Experiences of an officer of the 16th Light Dragoons in the Peninsular and Waterloo campaigns of the Napoleonic Wars.

SERGEANT BOURGOGNE by Adrien Bourgogne—With Napoleon's Imperial Guard in the Russian Campaign and on the Retreat from Moscow 1812 - 13.

SWORDS OF HONOUR by Henry Newbolt & Stanley L. Wood—The Careers of Six Outstanding Officers from the Napoleonic Wars, the Wars for India and the American Civil War, with dozens of illustrations by Stanley L. Wood.

SURTEES OF THE RIFLES by William Surtees—A Soldier of the 95th (Rifles) in the Peninsular campaign of the Napoleonic Wars.

ENSIGN BELL IN THE PENINSULAR WAR by George Bell—The Experiences of a young British Soldier of the 34th Regiment 'The Cumberland Gentlemen' in the Napoleonic wars.

HUSSAR IN WINTER by Alexander Gordon—A British Cavalry Officer during the retreat to Corunna in the Peninsular campaign of the Napoleonic Wars.

NAPOLEONIC WAR STORIES by Sir Arthur Quiller-Couch—Tales of soldiers, spies, battles & sieges from the Peninsular & Waterloo campaingns.

JOURNALS OF ROBERT ROGERS OF THE RANGERS by Robert Rogers—The exploits of Rogers & the Rangers in his own words during 1755-1761 in the French & Indian War.

KERSHAW'S BRIGADE VOLUME 1 by D. Augustus Dickert—Manassas, Seven Pines, Sharpsburg (Antietam), Fredricksburg, Chancellorsville, Gettysburg, Chickamauga, Chattanooga, Fort Sanders & Bean Station..

KERSHAW'S BRIGADE VOLUME 2 by D. Augustus Dickert—At the wilderness, Cold Harbour, Petersburg, The Shenandoah Valley and Cedar Creek.

A TIGER ON HORSEBACK by L. March Phillips—The Experiences of a Trooper & Officer of Rimington's Guides - The Tigers - during the Anglo-Boer war 1899 - 1902.

AVAILABLE ONLINE AT
www.leonaur.com
AND OTHER GOOD BOOK STORES

www.ingramcontent.com/pod-product-compliance
Lightning Source LLC
Chambersburg PA
CBHW031623160426
43196CB00006B/248